# Spiritual Disciplines 101

## pathway to God

Beacon Hill Press of Kansas City
Kansas City, Missouri

**Library of Congress Cataloging-in-Publication Data**

Spiritual disciplines 101 : pathway to God.
    p. cm.
  ISBN 0-8341-2214-6 (pbk.)
  1. Spiritual life—Christianity.  I. Title: Spiritual disciplines one hundred one.
  BV4501.3.S662 2005
  248—dc22

                                                                2005003001

10   9   8   7   6   5   4   3   2   1

# CONTENTS

# PREFACE

God can touch us in so many ways. Tender verses read or sung, the heartfelt prayer, the servant's hand, the well-worn journal—all these and more are avenues of God's transforming love. Throughout the life of the Church believers have opened themselves up to their divine Lord with these practices. Some called them acts of devotion; others called them disciplines and means of grace. They are points of contact with God—settings where we make ourselves available to His ever-available Self.

*Spiritual Disciplines 101* is an invitation to explore these practices with the help of experienced guides. The contributors to these pages include pastors, lay leaders, and educators.* Together they will introduce you to a variety of activities; some you may be familiar with, and others you may find quite new. As you read, you may discover that even the familiar contain vistas you have only just glimpsed.

Start with chapter 1, "Spiritual Disciplines: From Legalism to Liberty," by Steve Harper. This provides a general introduction to the disciplines and explains

---

*Many of these chapters are expansions of articles originally published in *Holiness Today,* the denominational periodical for the Church of the Nazarene. The contributions by James Earl Massey and Janine Tartaglia-Metcalf were originally chapters in other publications, and the chapter by Steve Harper was written especially for this volume.

how to approach them. Then peruse the book. Read the chapters in order, or skip to one that strikes your interest. After you have made your way through most of the text, prayerfully meditate on which practices you would like to try. Consider which ones will help you the most in your spiritual progress. You may want to take a chance and try the least comfortable for a time. Sometimes these fit the very areas where God's transformative love can work wonders, stretching and shaping you in marvelous Christlike ways.

The practices described in *Spiritual Disciplines 101* will make excellent additions to your spiritual-growth repertoire. Allow them to become a part of your quest for the transformed life. Let them be tools through which God can challenge, mold, and conform you to the image of His Son. Before long you may find that using these means of grace will result in you yourself becoming a means of grace to those around you. When this happens, you will probably discover very soon that even greater blessings are just around the corner.

# Spiritual Disciplines: From Legalism to Liberty

## steve harper

I cringe every time I hear someone say, "You need to live a disciplined life." After nearly 40 years as a pastor and professor, I've observed how many different ways people define the phrase "the disciplined life," and frankly, some of them are quite foreign to the essence of Christian faith and life. Almost every definition, even a good one, has to be approached with a wider view and set in a larger framework than the phrase alone contains. That's what I want to provide for you in this chapter—a broader perspective that will invite and enable you to use the spiritual disciplines in ways that will make you a more effective disciple of Jesus. Living a disciplined life is essential, but *how* you do that is as important as what you actually end up doing.[1]

For some of us, the problem begins with the word "discipline." We have associated it with the idea of punishment. We all have memories of parents and teachers having to "discipline" us because we had done something wrong. We can still hear their voices echoing in our minds, "OK, now you've done it. I'm going to have to discipline you." So, what happens when we come to the phrase "the disciplined life" with those kinds of memories? You know the answer—we draw back. We hesitate. We're not sure we want to go through another punitive process.

That's why I prefer to use the term "means of grace" as a synonym for spiritual disciplines. We all recognize our need for grace. Few people really believe they are self-sufficient. From the first day we seriously considered whether or not to accept Christ, we have understood ourselves to be in need of grace. But sometimes, we need help in understanding how the grace of God flows into our lives, and how we pattern ourselves so we can receive that grace. In parts of the Christian tradition, the phrase "means of grace" has been used rather than "spiritual disciplines" precisely as a way to understand them as means (not ends) by which we open ourselves to the grace of God. As I've taught about the spiritual disciplines, I have met people for whom this simple shift of phrase makes all the difference in how they view and practice a disciplined life.

The term "discipline" can also be problematic because it is equated with the system a leader uses for producing it. Unfortunately, there are unhealthy leaders who use the phrase "spiritual disciplines," but what they really mean is "being spiritual like I am."[2] They have a preconceived notion of what true devotion is, and it is almost always remarkably like the life they are living! It is a short step from defining your personal spirituality as "normative" to then creating a process that tries to make others like yourself, rather than guide them to be like Christ. I have known people who have been "de-formed" by pastors and teachers who had a "my way or the highway" view of the spiritual life. I have known unhealthy leaders who have built entire ministries (and the buildings that go with them) on little more than a self-centered view of "how things ought to be."

Once again, the term "means of grace" can help us. It moves us away from a leader-centered process to a Christ-centered process. It is God's grace that we need, not the alleged superiority of another's experience. We worship and serve a God who creates, not one who clones. We can learn from the example of others, when those examples are genuine and healthy. But we are never to "become" what someone else is. Practicing the spiritual disciplines will not suffocate your God-given uniqueness; it will release it. As the contemporary chorus puts it, "This is the air I breathe. / Your holy presence, living in me."

A third problem with the term "discipline" is that it can deteriorate into legalism. We can be taught or self-deceived into thinking that when we have adopted a cer-

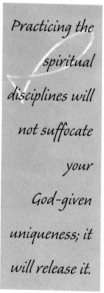

*Practicing the spiritual disciplines will not suffocate your God-given uniqueness; it will release it.*

tain list of spiritual disciplines, we are good Christians. We can use the list as a kind of litmus test that we always pass and then use to declare that we have "arrived." Without our intending it (at least most of the time), we can experience the erosion of our Christian walk into the keeping of "rules and regulations" given by a God who is more interested in our obedience than our love—a God who is more a lawgiver than a loving Father, a God who is ready to pounce on offenders more than to pronounce forgiveness when we confess our sins.

There are so many things wrong with this view of "discipline," I cannot write out everything associated with it.[3] The serious theological problem is that it turns the Christian life into one of "works" rather than one of faith. Everything depends on us—on our being sure that we have developed the "correct" list and that we are keeping it perfectly. Over the years, I have lost count of the number of defeated saints who thought they had to get it right all the time; otherwise, God was "mad" at them. Whenever we practice the spiritual disciplines as a way to "prove" our spirituality, we have become entrapped in legalism, and we are in desperate need of liberty.

We could go on to list other misconceptions that surround the term "living a disciplined life," but it is not the point of this chapter to describe the problems as much as it is to propose how we move beyond them to a proper use of spiritual disciplines (the means of grace) in our Christian walk. However, I hope that some of you who read this chapter will be comforted as you realize you may have been the recipient of bad teaching and/or "deformative" experiences in relation to the spiritual disciplines. If so, I hope you will celebrate that at this very moment you are on the journey from legalism to liberty, and the spiritual disciplines are God-given practices to enable that to happen in your life. But as I said at the beginning of this chapter, we need a larger framework and wider view if this is to be so. The rest of the chapter will attempt to provide that. I will do it through a series of related words that enable us to understand and practice the spiritual disciplines in a healthy way.

### disciple

The spiritual disciplines will never be what they are intended to be until we understand and deeply acknowledge that we are "disciples" of Jesus. This is our primary identity as Christians, and without it the spiritual disciplines will always appear as a "tack on" to whatever other views of ourselves we have. I have worked with many frustrated pastors who lament, "I can't seem to get my people interested in the spiritual disciplines." Often this is because many people operate more with a "member mentality" than a "disciple mentality." As long as this is the case, the call to live a disciplined life will fall on deaf ears. As one member crassly told his pastor, "Why should I do that? I'm a member in good standing in this congregation. What more is there?"

But everything changes when we realize that the primary word to describe our Christian life is "disciple." The word means learner. It means follower. It means someone else is in control, and our task is to dispose our hearts and position our lives in ways that will enable us to see Jesus more clearly, love Him more dearly, and follow Him more nearly—day by day. When this not only dawns upon us but also sinks deeply into us, it will make perfect sense to "practice the presence of God" through the use of spiritual disciplines.[4]

But something else happens when we adopt the word "disciple" as the primary identifier of our lives. We find that this view coincides with the deepest desire of our hearts. We are made in the image of God, and as Augustine[5] said, our hearts are restless until they rest in God. To live the life of a disciple is to live the life we have always wanted to live.[6] When we live as disciples, our hearts exclaim, "For this I was made!" And out of that exclamation will come a willingness to practice the spiritual disciplines in whatever ways will make us better followers of the Master. I have watched this happen for decades, as people experience the movement of a "disciplined life" from something they think is "outside" (i.e., imposed) to one that is "inside" (i.e., something invited). The difference is startling, and it all hinges on who we understand ourselves to be.

> There is no "one size fits all" model for being a disciple.

Closely related to this is the important realization that there is no "one size fits all" model for being a disciple. When you study the list of the first apostles (Mark 3:16-19), you see how different each of them was, and if you follow that with how tradition says they were used in the Early Church, the point is clear that God delights to use us as we are made in creation, not simply in re-creation.

Our personality traits and talents combine with our spiritual gifts to make us men and women who will be used by God in an amazing variety of ways. And when it comes to the spiritual disciplines, it means we will not all make use of the same ones, and we will even practice the same ones in different ways. The end result is a "disciple" who brings joy to God's heart.

## discipline

When we understand who we are, God's beloved children, who live as faithful disciples, then we know how to begin adopting the means to become who we say we are. And that brings us to "discipline," not as punishment, but as disposition. When we know we are disciples, we are at the place where we can bring the word "discipline" back into the picture, this time as God intends for it to be.

There are two primary images in this regard. First, Jesus says in John 15 that we are branches and He is the vine. And one of the key elements in that image is that branches have to be pruned so that they may bear more fruit. If we are not careful, we will misread the word "pruned" in the same way we sometimes misread the word "discipline." So, let me write it out again: we are pruned *so that we may bear more fruit.* If we see ourselves as disciples, isn't that exactly what we want —to "bear more fruit" for Jesus? Of course it is, and in that context we come to understand discipline as the disposing of our lives so that Christ can lead us where He wants us to go and do with us what He wants to do. This does not mean that every form of discipline will be neat, quick, clean, easy, and painless. There are times when discipline is the toughest thing God asks us to do. The difference now is that it is set in an entirely different frame of reference: our desire to please God and our willingness to have God engage us to our maximum potential.

The second image is the mind of Christ in Phil. 2:5-11. Here, the idea of discipline is one of servanthood.[7] Our use of the spiritual disciplines is our multifaceted way of asking God day after day, "How can I serve You?"

I'm told that every morning the late Frank Laubach began his day with this prayer: "Lord, what are You doing in the world today that I can help You with?" That is the prayer of someone who understands he is a servant. Discipline, therefore, is not about doing what we don't want to do—it is doing the thing we most want to do—serving Jesus in ways that glorify God.

Both these images connect us to the single idea of surrender.[8] Rooted in Paul's exhortation for Roman Christians to present themselves to God as living sacrifices (12:1), the concept winds its way through the history of Christian spirituality. Whatever else being a "living sacrifice" may mean, it surely means that, unlike dead sacrifices that could only be offered once, we can offer ourselves repeatedly to God. The practical act of daily submitting ourselves to God through the use of spiritual disciplines leads to the deeper surrender of our lives. One of the ways I like to say it is,

*Discipline, therefore, is not about doing what we don't want to do—it is doing the thing we most want to do—serving Jesus in ways that glorify God.*

"God does not ask us to have a devotional tim
calls us to live a devotional life." Of course, we will so
aside specific times to engage in the practice of the
disciplines, but our goal is a deeper attitude (what we
are calling "discipline")—one that prays, "Take my life,
and let it be / Consecrated, Lord, to Thee." Our lives
are now in God's hands; our hearts are now disposed
to discern and do God's will. Out of this fundamental
shift in attitude (from selfishness to surrender), we
view and practice the spiritual disciplines in a radical-
ly different way.

## disciplines

Now we are at the place where we can use the
word that appears in the title of this chapter. I hope
you can see why I said at the beginning that we must
have a broader perspective and a larger framework before we can understand where the spiritual disciplines
fit into the scheme of things. And I repeat the point
that I made earlier: if we try to skip over the concepts
of "disciple" and "discipline," we end up trying to require people to do things they are not properly motivated or disposed to do. But when these two ideas are
deeply rooted in us, we are at the point where the use
of spiritual disciplines will enable us to produce what
others have called "the life of God in the human soul."

We will most likely begin our use of spiritual disciplines within the particular faith tradition in which we
find ourselves. That is as it should be, for every tradition teaches the disciplines differently—both in relation to what they are and how they are to be used. One
of the first things we should do is to find out what "the

Christian spiritual life" means in our own denominational or parachurch history.[9] But as we do this, it will
become apparent that our predecessors have drunk
from wells that preceded their own times and predat-
ed the creation of the church to which we belong. It is
impossible to study the Christian spiritual life and
stay encased in one tradition. Consequently, we will
discover that many streams have converged to produce both our particular tradition and the larger
Christian tradition in which we stand.[10]

As we broaden our exposure to these other
sources, we will discover that each of the spiritual disciplines have been practiced by different people in
different ways. Take prayer, for example. We will find
that some have prayed mostly out loud, while others
have prayed in silence. We will find some who have
prayed with prayer books and others who have prayed
only extemporaneously. We will find some who have
emphasized praise, while others have focused on in-
tercession. We will find some preferring personal
prayer and others who pray mainly in groups.

And what does this do for us? For one thing, it
gives us a bigger picture of a specific spiritual discipline than we could ever have if we defined or limited
it to what we know from our particular tradition. For
another thing, it shows that we have much room in
which to move in order to discover how to practice a
particular spiritual discipline for ourselves. But perhaps most importantly, it ends forever the notion that
"we do it right" while others "do it wrong." It elimi-
nates the narcissistic spirituality we referred to at the
beginning of the chapter. We come to see what God

has wanted us to see ever since the author of Hebrews wrote that "we are surrounded by such a great cloud of witnesses" (12:1). And we find to our delight and benefit that making friends with various members of that "cloud" creates a stronger spirituality, and one that it is more nearly Christlike. It means that we will always have an element of the classical, historic, and lasting quality of the spiritual life as we practice the spiritual disciplines.

With all this before us, we are at the place where some indication of what the spiritual disciplines actually are will be helpful. I have deliberately shied away from giving you a list, lest you think any such list covers them all. In fact, even at this point in the chapter, I prefer you to begin the list with a view of their role: disciplines to strengthen us inwardly, disciplines to strengthen us outwardly, and disciplines to strengthen us corporately.[11] With these basic categories in place, Foster provides some disciplines for each dimension as follows:

The Inward Disciplines
    Meditation
    Prayer
    Fasting
    Study
The Outward Disciplines
    Simplicity
    Solitude
    Submission
    Service
The Corporate Disciplines
    Confession

> *The spiritual disciplines are intended to be channels for the grace of God to enable us to live the lives we have to live at any particular moment.*

Worship
Guidance
Celebration

There are two very important things to keep in mind as you read this list—both of which Richard Foster shared with me personally years ago. First, this list (and any other one, for that matter) is not exhaustive. And second, no Christian will practice all 12 disciplines equally well all the time. The point is this: the spiritual disciplines are intended to be channels for the grace of God to enable us to live the lives we have to live at any particular moment. From this list alone, you can see how different spiritual disciplines could facilitate a particular kind of life experience. Because the Holy Spirit is working in and through all the disciplines, we can trust God to "activate" our use of any of them to make us more like Christ in whatever situations we find ourselves. Some of the disciplines will be rather permanent, and we will practice them almost daily. Others may come and go as the occasions for them appear and/or the need for them arises. The end result will be what Jesus said, "I have come that they may have life, and that they may have it more abundantly" (John 10:10, NKJV).

## discipleship

I really like this last word. I often tell my students that "discipleship is two or more disciples in the same boat." Our practice of the spiritual disciplines has brought us to a grand place—the place where we can relate to and benefit from one another. The practice of the spiritual disciplines was never meant to foster a "Me and Jesus" lifestyle. Our use of the means of grace is designed to bring us into closer fellowship with other disciples—into what John Wesley referred to as Christian conference.

This idea goes all the way back into the earliest phases of Christianity. Most especially, Jesus himself could not live His life on earth without doing it in a community of apostles and friends. Pentecost happened when the believers were all together in one place (Acts 2:1). And nearer to the end of the New Testament era, the writer of Hebrews warned Christians not to neglect "the assembling of ourselves together" (10:25, NKJV). And Paul's entire strategy was to establish communities of faith throughout the Roman Empire and tie them together with common stewardship and missional responsibilities.

A clear understanding of "discipleship"—that is, viewed as Christian community—is where a proper practice of spiritual disciplines will take us. I often say to my students, "Is the word 'church' singular or plural?" If they answer according to grammar, the answer is singular. But when we answer biblically and theologically, the answer is always plural. And it is the formation of a perspective that understands that this community is always larger than the particular part of the Body of Christ in which I happen to be a member.

I've discovered that one of the most practical benefits of this kind of vision is that it saves me from a myopic view of the Christian life. I have to confess—it would be so much easier to create my own spiritual life and then settle comfortably into it. I would not have to deal with others or be influenced by them. I'm not the first to feel this way. Dorotheos of Gaza, a sixth-century leader of a monastic community, became concerned that fellow monks were grumbling too much about having to put up with each other and their irritating practices. Some of them thought they could love God "better" if they went back to living as hermits. Dorotheos told them flat out they were wrong. He asked them to visualize the world as a big circle with God at the center. He then asked them to see themselves somewhere on the circumference, along with the other members of the monastery—indeed, with everyone else in the world. "Imagine now," he said, "that there are straight lines connecting every human life on the circumference to God at the center. Can't you see that there is no way to move toward God without drawing closer to other people, and no way to approach other people without coming nearer to God?"[12]

Our practice of the spiritual disciplines will make us holier, healthier, happier, and better connected to the rest of the Body of Christ. In fact, I personally believe that our use of the means of grace will create a desire to know as many different kinds of Christians as we can, precisely because

> *Our practice of the spiritual disciplines will make us holier, healthier, happier, and better connected to the rest of the Body of Christ.*

each person will magnify and clarify our understanding and experience of God. Our use of spiritual disciplines will generate a journey to find as many brothers and sisters in the family of God as we can. And one of our great joys will be to pass our years being marvelously blessed by a host of men and women we would not have met if we had limited our exposure to those "like us."

Books are interesting things. They contain words, but they are most valuable when they enable us to "see" things. I hope you can "see" what I have been trying to write about in this chapter. Can you "see" how God views the spiritual disciplines and how God intends for you to practice them? Have you been able to see that "discipline," far from being punitive, is actually an expression of the very kind of life we want to live if we see ourselves as disciples of Jesus? Will you now be able to use the spiritual disciplines to make the journey from legalism to liberty? If you can honestly answer yes to these questions, I will have written this chapter the way I set out to write it. Over the years, I have heard Richard Foster say repeatedly, "The spiritual disciplines enable us to do what needs to be done, when it needs to be done." There is nothing more liberating than that.

## notes

1. This chapter is only an introduction to a much bigger subject, so one of the things I will do is to provide you with notes to take you beyond my own thoughts. In terms of the "how" of spiritual disciplines (not merely the "what"), I would encourage you to read Dallas Willard's *The Spirit of the Disciplines* (San Francisco: HarperSanFrancisco, 1988).

2. See Gary L. McIntosh and Samuel D. Rima Sr., *Overcoming the Dark Side of Leadership* (Grand Rapids: Baker Books, 1997), especially chapter 8, "The Narcissistic Leader," 94-103.

3. David Seamands, *Healing Grace* (Wheaton, Ill.: Victor Books, 1988) is one of the best books available to help you break free from the trap of performance-oriented Christianity.

4. Richard Foster's *Celebration of Discipline* (San Francisco: Harper and Row, 1978—with subsequent revisions) is written from this point of view. They can only exist in the lives of "deep people"—people who are disciples, not dabblers, in the spiritual journey.

5. The great theologian, bishop, and church father (d. A.D. 430).

6. John Ortberg, *The Life You've Always Wanted: Spiritual Disciplines for Ordinary People* (Grand Rapids: Zondervan, 2002).

7. Dennis F. Kinlaw, *The Mind of Christ* (Nappannee, Ind.: Francis Asbury Press, 1998).

8. Jean-Pierre de Caussade, *The Sacrament of the Present Moment* (New York: Harper and Row, 1966). This classic, originally published in 1741, remains one of the best books to read for understanding what the life of surrender really is. A newer work is E. Stanley Jones' *Victory Through Surrender* (Nashville: Abingdon, 1966).

9. For example, I am a United Methodist, and so I want to stand in the best spiritual-formation tradition I can as a Wesleyan Christian. I have tried to help Christians in my tradition do this through my books *Devotional Life in the Wesleyan Tradition: A Workbook* (Nashville: Upper Room Books, 1995) and *Prayer and Devotional Life for United Methodists* (Nashville: Abingdon, 1999). Books like this are available for many of the traditions within Roman Catholic, Orthodox, and Protestant churches.

10. Richard Foster has given us a great gift in his book *Streams of Living Water* (San Francisco: HarperSanFrancisco, 1998), as he shows us how we can celebrate and benefit from the great traditions of the Christian faith.

11. Use Richard Foster's *Celebration of Discipline,* previous-

ly cited, to continue to develop the disciplines along these lines. I have not found any better way to organize them than this. Also, Dallas Willard in his book *The Spirit of the Disciplines* organizes the disciplines according to those that help us be more "reflective" and those that enable us to be more "active." I particularly like this approach because it helps us see that the disciplines contribute to the creation of the kind of life God wants us to live—that holy blend of contemplation and action.

12. Adapted from *Dorotheos of Gaza: Discourses and Sayings,* trans. Eric P. Wheeler (Kalamazoo, Mich.: Cistercian Publications, 1977), 138-39. In this same vein, you will enjoy Roberta C. Bondi's book *Memories of God* (Nashville: Abingdon, 1995), 200-202.

Dr. Steve Harper is vice president and professor of spiritual formation at the Florida campus of Asbury Theological Seminary in Orlando, Florida.

# THE POWERHOUSE OF PRAYER AND SCRIPTURE

## rebecca laird

**The London taxi dropped us** on City Road outside of Wesley's Chapel in London only minutes before closing time. A guide hurriedly pointed out details of interest in the simple chapel and in an adjoining room offered to let us play the manual pipe organ owned by Charles Wesley, John's hymn-writing brother. I imagined the place full of the robust voices of enthusiastic 18th-century Christians singing "O for a Thousand Tongues to Sings."

We were then escorted to the simple backyard cemetery where John Wesley is buried. We asked to see the adjoining house where Wesley lived most of his adult life only to discover it already had been locked and alarmed. Then the guide who held the keys looked down at his hands and said with a wry smile, "If you arrived at 4:45 P.M., you were 10 minutes earlier than most Americans. Come and I'll show you Wesley's study and bedroom."

We walked up a narrow flight of stairs and into a small study with wooden shuttered windows and shelves with leather-bound books. Nothing was cordoned off. This did not seem like a museum but rather like the room of a greatly revered yet departed teacher whose belongings were still in the places where he left them. After we looked at the desk and discussed some of the books on the shelves, Bob, our guide, said, "Follow me to the powerhouse of Methodism." We followed him past Wesley's simple bed and chair and into a tiny closet-sized prayer room. The shutters leaked light, and the room must have been hot in the summer and terribly cold and damp in the winter.

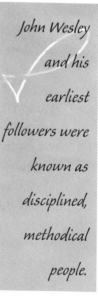

*John Wesley and his earliest followers were known as disciplined, methodical people.*

Despite the Spartan nature of the room, Wesley rose daily at 4:30 A.M. and sat in the wooden straight-backed chair in the back corner by the window. Pride in early rising was not Wesley's goal; he simply was committed to giving his first attentions each day to God. Before dawn, he faced an altar stand that held an open Bible. A simple white kneeling cushion was tucked beneath. For hours each morning alone in this prayer corner, Wesley prayed, read Scripture, and sang. Bob, our guide, said, "The power that helped Methodism change the world was plugged in here."

John Wesley and his earliest followers

were known as disciplined, methodical people. They understood that while God alone transforms the deep recesses of the human heart, we are called to engage in repeated, physical bodily behaviors and spiritual acts that over time God uses to reorder the interior recesses of the heart. Rising early, sitting in the same chair, kneeling at the same altar, using the eyes to read and voice to sing, and meeting often with others were all acts that put a person's life in a posture to hear and be of use to God. These activities are our "responsive participation in God's forgiving and empowering grace."[1]

## wesleyan spiritual hallmarks

All Christian traditions emphasize discipline, regular Bible study, and prayer. What makes Wesleyan spirituality distinct is the delicate balance held between beliefs, actions, and the condition of the heart. Wesleyan spirituality holds three spiritual truths in tension: Orthodoxy, or right belief, is important but will not save on its own. Orthopraxis, or right action, is essential, but doing good devoid of love counts for little. Orthokardia, or having a right heart, provides the wellspring of positive love. When a person has a right heart, his or her behaviors can be traced back to a motive of love and this is what it means to live a sanctified, holy Christian life.

To live out this "motive of love," we prime the pump, open the floodgate, work the soil, center down, engage in spiritual disciplines or practices—choose your metaphor—so that God's gracious love can do its work in each of us. We must do our part, yet Wesley made it plain in his sermon titled "The Means of

Grace" that it is always God, not the discipline or action, that does the work. Wesley wanted it to be very clear that the means (spiritual practices or disciplines) were just means unless the Spirit of God blew through them to quicken us to spiritual sensitivity. He wrote, "Before you use any means [of grace], let it be deeply impressed on your soul,—there is no *power* in this. It is, in itself, a poor, dead, empty thing: Separate from God, it is a dry leaf, a shadow. Neither is there any *merit* in my using this; nothing intrinsically pleasing to God; nothing whereby I deserve any favour at His hands, no, not a drop of water to cool my tongue. But, because God bids, therefore I do; because he directs me to wait in this way, therefore here I wait for His free mercy, whereof cometh my salvation."[2]

*We engage in spiritual disciplines because we want more of God.*

We engage in spiritual disciplines because we want more of God. We follow the example of Jesus' life and trust that God has shown us through Scripture and the empowered holy lives of those who have gone before us how to grow in grace.

If we could ask John Wesley to tell us more about how to go about this, he would probably point us to his "General Rules"—the three basic "guideposts" or "railings" that he defined for the earliest Methodist societies, groups of people who were mutually committed to spiritual growth. He would advise us to avoid "evil in every kind," do "good of every possible sort," and attend "upon all the ordinances of God."[3] These ordinances of God are the "means of grace," which as we have seen is how Wesley alternately and eloquently referred to spiritual disciplines or spiritual practices. The means of grace include spiritual practices that are "instituted," meaning that they were evident in the life of Jesus. Prayer and searching the Scriptures, fasting and partaking of the Lord's Supper, living life among a small group of faithful people—these are certainly among the instituted disciplines. Most of these are "works of piety" or devotion that are done privately or within the boundaries of one's community of faith.

There are other means of grace called "prudential" ones, meaning that the church over the ages has found these disciplines worthy of repeating. For Wesley most of the prudential means of grace were interpersonal "works of mercy" that required people to do good to benefit others in body and soul. Caring for the sick, feeding the poor, and serving those in material need are all prudential means of grace. These disciplines took the early Methodists, and will take any of us, far beyond the comfortable walls of home or church. These disciplines take us—as they did Wesley—into the neglected quarters of our world where people in great need are often found. Indeed, over time a hallmark of the Wesleyan movement was that it crossed economic and class divides, bringing people together out of love for Jesus Christ.

A Wesleyan spirituality is both individual and corporate. It requires us to care equally about our personal spiritual well-being and the health of the world. We are called to live full lives of faith, not just to give a tiny portion of our mornings to some devotional practice. Wesley knew that a real faith would be formed in community and would result in service to the world. When head and heart are connected in faith, the hands get involved in service.

Yet there has to be a starting place. We have to go back to the powerhouse and begin with the essentials —the spiritual bread and living water for our faith— daily prayer and searching the Scriptures. And if we are to follow in the Wesleyan way, we will sing.

## daily prayer

Wesley and his societies were well-known for keeping each other accountable by regularly asking direct spiritual questions of each other. In regards to prayer, he asked many questions like the following to help keep people's prayer life on track:

- Do you pray every morning and evening?
- Are you as faithful about your prayer time as you are about your appointments or meetings?
- How do you plan ahead to secure time with God in prayer?[4]

Wesley was broadminded about prayer. He wrote in *A Plain Account of Christian Perfection,* "All that a Christian does, even in eating and sleeping, is prayer, when it is done in simplicity, according to the order of God, without either adding to or diminishing from it by his own choice."[5]

The way to become faithful in prayer is to set a time and vigorously keep it. Wesley's own early morning prayer time proves the efficacy of his method. Once the time is set, here are some simple suggestions on how to pray.

*Find a way daily to be in God's presence.* Wesley

*Time of day doesn't matter as much as regularity and the condition of your heart when you pray.*

fixed his first thoughts on God each morning. Throughout the ages, many have found that prayer in the early hours of the day focuses the rest of the day. But a minority of people pray at other times. Time of day doesn't matter as much as regularity and the condition of your heart when you pray. So pray. Address your requests, praise, need for forgiveness, and intercessions for others through prayer.

*Pick a posture of attentiveness.* Praying requires attentiveness. Allow your body to be in a receptive posture of prayer. This can be kneeling or sitting upright in a chair. It's not a good idea to fully recline to pray, as you may find it harder to stay focused. Wesley was a straight-backed man who prayed often sitting upright or while riding on horseback. He shows us that we can pray when alone or while on the road, but we need to be intentional and focused. Most people who are consistent in their prayer discover that a specific location and physical posture helps them pray. Some kneel by the bedside. Others sit in a chair with their feet grounded on the floor. A few find that walking helps the body and the mind work together in prayer. Often in the church where I serve, I discover people have come to our chapel to sit on the wooden pews and pray in the quiet beauty and light of the stained-glass windows. Praying beneath a tree on a grassy lawn is fine too. Whatever your preferred posture, just allow your body and your heart to be in a humble and receptive stance before God. The words we say are vehicles to express our gratitude, joys, and concerns, but God accepts our prayers based on the condition of the heart that offers them—not the eloquence with which they are spoken.

*Pray in various ways.* Prayer is an ongoing conversation with God. And like any lasting dialogue, what is shared varies. Prayer can be said privately in God's presence alone. Prayer can also be said in the company of family, friends, fellow Christians, and strangers alike. Prayers can be spontaneous, when we allow the concerns of our hearts to be expressed by the heartfelt words of our mouth. Prayers can also be read or recited from the Psalms and from the Christian tradition. Prayers found in the Book of Common Prayer or contained in a formal liturgy or prayer collections are important for the praying Christian. Wesley felt that written prayers—those put down on paper by others or penned personally—combat a wandering mind. Adding our assent to the prayers of those who have gone before us brings us into the company of saints when we pray and also helps us to pray about the broader concerns of God when we are mute or blinded by our own views and need help in widening our hearts. Formal prayers remind us to both thank God and confess our sins. The key to using written formal prayers is to remember to pray them, not just to scan them or mumble them mindlessly. Sometimes praying aloud helps. Prayer of any kind requires that we show

*The key to using written formal prayers is to remember to pray them, not just to scan them or mumble them mindlessly.*

up honestly and humbly with mind, body, and spirit before God.

*Leave room for silence.* In any relationship each party does a good share of the communicating, and silence punctuates the words. Too many words and too many concerns can plug the prayer channel. God commands us to "be still, and know that I am God" (Ps. 46:10). When we are awake, aware, and quiet in God's presence, we may hear God's voice in powerful ways. Words are not necessary at all to pray. Silence before God is a profound way of aligning our hearts to the stillness with which God speaks. If your life is full of noise and God seems to be far away, take some time and find a corner of space and time to breathe deeply and inhale the love of God that is always available even when we can't see it, hear it, or feel it.

Silence is not a familiar friend to many in our hurried, noisy culture. If you find silence awkward, start slowly. Set aside three minutes or so and sit before God. If you need something to focus on, light a candle. You might also try to focus your attention on your breathing. As you inhale, think to yourself, "Breathe in the love of God." As you exhale, focus on, "Breathe out the love of God." Let the simple act of paying attention to your breathing help you savor the presence of God and the gift of life for a short time.

*Live a life of love.* Wesley traveled constantly and preached an amazing number of times. His was a busy life. He understood that prayer requires regular quiet time but that it encompasses so much more. He advised people to live a life of love and explained that prayer is a practical thing. For "souls filled with love, the desire to please God is a continual prayer."[6]

## search the scriptures

Some of Wesley's questions to his fellow believers about "Searching the Scriptures" were these:

- Are you reading constantly, a part of every day, regularly?
- Are you reading the entire Bible in order?
- Are you reading seriously, with prayer before and after, and immediately practicing what you learn?[7]

Centuries after Wesley, we must also approach Scripture as our primary guide to life. John Wesley called himself a "Bible bigot." By that he declared himself to be a person whose ultimate standard was Holy Scripture. That doesn't mean that Wesley read only the Bible. On the contrary he was an outstanding scholar who read materials spanning from ancient sources to those contemporary to his time. He read books by people he agreed with and those that he did not. The Bible provided Wesley's lens and focus, while his theology and spiritual understanding was synthesized from many varied sources. So prioritize the Bible and start reading. Here are some suggestions for a balanced use of Scripture.

*Read reverently and expectantly.* The Bible is to be read as a living source of spiritual wisdom and encouragement. Just as you would hang on to the words of a trusted friend who advised you on the important aspects of life, savor the Bible. It is not to be read on the run or when distracted.

*When we read anticipating a word from God, the Spirit can guide us to the truth we need for daily living.*

*Look to it to form and reform your heart and actions.* In Scripture you will see the faults, sins, and hardness of heart that others have faced. So, too, you will find out your own sins written in clear type. You may weep at the continual record of God's forgiveness, mercy, and blessing. Give yourself a daily dose of sacred reading. Let a small portion of the Bible be sustenance for your soul.

*Pray for illumination as you read.* Ask God to teach you what you need to learn and for an open, malleable spirit. Wesley believed that Scripture could be understood only by the illumination of the Holy Spirit that made it God-inspired in the first place. When we read anticipating a word from God, the Spirit can guide us to the truth we need for daily living.

*Start with the Psalms and Gospels.* If you are new to Bible reading, it's best to begin with the prayers of the people of God found in the Psalms and the stories of the life of Jesus found in the Gospels. Wesley encouraged people to read and meditate on a passage from both the Old and New Testaments each morning and evening. There are good guides that follow the common lectionary that can help you read systematically through the Old and New Testaments. You might want to start with a small portion of Scripture and, when a word, phrase, or idea captures your mind or puzzles you, stop. Offer that portion of Scripture as a prayer to God. Meditate on the words. (To meditate means to let it rest in your mind and heart as you slowly let the truth of the words penetrate beyond your intellect and into your heart, which is the seat of your will and actions.) Some people like to have a Bible dictionary nearby to look up new words or names, but only do this after you've allowed the Scripture to water your soul. By itself, head knowledge about Scripture rarely changes your heart, but when Scripture softens you from head to toe, you will truly be a living sacrifice that pleases God.

Wesley also recommended finishing a time of Scripture reading with prayer so that what was read may be written on our hearts and turned into positive action.

*Study Scripture allowing the views of others to help.* Bible study with others is where it is appropriate to dig more deeply into the theological meanings, word studies, cultural ideas, and ethical challenges raised in the biblical text. Studying the Bible with others helps us to widen the personal lens that each of us brings when reading the Bible alone. There are many layers of meaning and an inexhaustible supply of wisdom to be found in Scripture study. If we can't study with others face-to-face, utilizing biblical reference books brings us into contact with the thoughts and knowledge of others.

Wesley understood that a solid Christian faith was built on a sound and full knowledge of Scripture. He wrote *Explanatory Notes* for the Old and New Testaments. He compiled his commentary notes expecting that ordinary Christians could and should study the Bible on their own. His notes show he read the various views held by others, and he learned from them all, whether theological friend or foe. To urge others on to effective study, he posed some questions each faithful student of the Bible could ask:

- Am I reading the Bible in a way that brings me into contact with the whole of it?
- Do I read in large enough portions to see isolated passages in a larger context?
- Do I use responsible aids to add the insights of others to my own study of God's Word?[8]

*Read comprehensively.* Wesley was ever a man to develop patterns for spiritual growth. In his own Bible reading he devised the following method. Read daily, both morning and evening. Read with a singleness of purpose to know God's will. Compare scripture with scripture so that no one passage is taken separately from the whole Word of God. Read prayerfully so that the Holy Spirit can speak through Scripture. Read resolutely, and immediately put what you've learned into practice.[9] Finally, Wesley believed that the Word of God would illumine and teach us, but the learning was never just for us alone. We are to share our insights and knowledge with others.

## sing out your praise and worship

For Protestants of many varieties, singing is almost as natural as breathing. Singing is one of our primary devotional practices and a preferred way of praying. Through song we praise God, we invoke God's presence and blessing, and we sing love songs to the God of our hearts.

The people that would one day be called "Methodists" for their methodical spiritual practices and strategies of small-group and church organization also have been labeled as those people who learned their faith and beliefs by singing them! Wesley gave his followers simple and clear direction for singing to encourage the spiritual aspects of singing. He wrote the following suggestions in a hymnal created in 1761.

I.  Learn these tunes before you learn any others; afterwards learn as many as you please.

II.  Sing them exactly as they are printed here, without altering or mending them at all; and if you have learned to sing them otherwise, unlearn it as soon as you can.

III.  Sing all. See that you join with the congregation as frequently as you can. Let not a slight degree of weakness or weariness hinder you. If it is a cross to you, take it up, and you will find it a blessing.

IV.  Sing lustily and with a good courage. Beware of singing as if you were half dead, or half asleep; but lift up your voice with strength. Be no more afraid of your voice now, nor more ashamed of its being heard, than when you sung the songs of Satan.

V.  Sing modestly. Do not bawl, so as to be heard above or distinct from the rest of the congregation, that you may not destroy the harmony; but strive to unite your voices together, so as to make one clear melodious sound.

VI.  Sing in time. Whatever time is sung, be sure to keep with it. Do not run before nor stay behind it; but attend close to the leading voices, and move therewith as exactly as you can; and take care not to sing too slow. This drawling way naturally steals on all who are lazy; and it is high time to drive it out from us, and sing all our tunes just as quick as we did at first.

VII. Above all sing spiritually. Have an eye to God in every word you sing. Aim at pleasing Him more than yourself, or any other creature. In order to do this attend strictly to the sense of what you sing, and see that your heart is not carried away with the sound, but offered to God continually; so shall your singing be such as the Lord will approve here, and reward you when he cometh in the clouds of heaven.[10]

Singing is certainly about staying on tune and savoring beautiful words and music, but it is also about taking in air and using it to give voice to our deeper yearnings. Music can and will unpack and break down hardened places inside of us. Singing also creates physical changes in us. As we sing, our breathing deepens and slows. Muscles often relax, skin temperatures change, and our emotions are unleashed. Our scattered attentions become focused. When we sing, we become centered—life-giving air moves into the centers of our bodies and returns as praise.

*When we sing, we become centered—life-giving air moves into the centers of our bodies and returns as praise.*

Wesley knew the spiritual benefits of singing. The power of sung prayers comes from its wholeheartedness as well as its physicality. When we sing as if our lives depended on it, we begin to sense that the words of our mouths have the power to bring us into the presence of God (who, of course, is ever-present even if we remain deaf to the divine activity around us).

If we want to know how to plug into God's power, the answer is clear. The powerhouse is found through daily prayer, regular study of Scripture, and whole-hearted singing. May we all find our own quiet corner and go there often so that our lives may be remembered as ones fueled by the power of God.

## notes

1. Randy Maddox, *Responsible Grace: John Wesley's Practical Theology* (Nashville: Kingswood Books/Abingdon Press, 1994), 192.

2. John Wesley, *The Works of John Wesley,* ed. Thomas Jackson, 3d ed. (1872; reprint, Peabody, Mass.: Hendrickson Publishers, 1984), 5:200-201.

3. Ibid., 8:270-71

4. Ibid., 322-24.

5. John Wesley, *A Plain Account of Christian Perfection* (1725-77; reprint, Kansas City: Beacon Hill Press of Kansas City, 1966), 109.

6. Ibid.

7. Wesley, *Works,* 8:323.

8. See Ibid., 8:323, 14:253.

9. See Ibid., 14:252-53.

10. From John Wesley's *Select Hymns* (1761).

Rebecca Laird is an ordained minister of the Church of the Nazarene serving on special assignment as associate for spiritual development at Central Presbyterian Church in Summit, New Jersey. She is coeditor with Michael Christensen of *The Heart of Henri Nouwen: His Words of Blessing* (Crossroad Publishers). This chapter is an expansion of an article first published in *Holiness Today,* January 2004.

# THE DISCIPLINE OF FASTING

## james earl massey

**There are times when voluntary** abstention from food can play an important role in our religious life. The voluntary discipline of fasting can distinctively prepare the Christian for deeper living and public service for God. The values of this discipline are so thoroughly documented in history that no one can legitimately raise a serious question about whether fasting is beneficial to a Christian's life.

### fasting in old testament times

The discipline of fasting was quite important during Old Testament times. Fasting was enjoined as a necessary part of the ritual for the national Day of Atonement. The nation of Israel was directed to observe fasting on that day by the Mosaic Law: "On the tenth day of this seventh month is the day of atonement; it shall be for you a time of holy convocation, and you shall afflict yourselves" (Lev. 23:27, RSV). The Hebrew word translated *you shall afflict* literally meant "to fast, to abstain from food for reasons of penitence and confession." To the young Israelite nation, no day was more sacred than the national Day of Atonement, and the observance of fasting was an indispensable requirement for that day. A severe penalty was exercised against disobedient offenders: "For whoever is not afflicted on this same day shall be cut off from his people" (Lev. 23:29, RSV).

Later prophetic writings show that at least four other national fast days were observed during the postexilic period. The references in Jeremiah (14:11-12; 36:4-8), Zechariah (7:5; 8:19), and Joel (2:12-15) suggest that, because of the national disaster of the fall of Jerusalem, fasting was enjoined for purposes of penitence and recollection of sins. Fasting helped the nation recall why the ruin had occurred. It reminded the nation of their need for obedience to God as His people. These national fasts obliged each Israelite to show penitence, grief, and recognition of the nation's need for God. The fasting was designed to cause each individual to face anew the will of God.

Numerous Old Testament passages suggest that fasting was a *penitential action,* part of the ritual of self-abasement in order to become acceptable before God. Fasting had to be motivated by this attitude. Isaiah condemns fasting that is not done in the spirit of true mourning and penitence (Isa. 58:3-5). Jeremiah laments Judah's impenitent fasting at a time when they were threatened by a devastating drought (Jer.

*Some Old Testament passages suggest that fasting was at times a preparatory action, a way of being readied for closeness with God.*

14:11-12). He later seeks to gain a hearing for his oracles during a day of national fasting, a time when he expected all ears to be open to God (cf. Jer. 36:4 ff.), "but they would not hear" (v. 31, RSV). By Jeremiah's time, the practice of fasting had become a cold observance, purely external, lacking in proper motivation. God promised to hear prayers backed by sincere fasting (Isa. 58:10) but warned that He would disregard hollow and cold practice of the observance.

Some Old Testament passages suggest that fasting was at times a *preparatory action,* a way of being readied for closeness with God. When done by someone truly seeking God, a penitential fast would help the worshiper return to God, while a preparatory fast would sensitize one to commune with God in depth. Joel 2:12-13 is an example of the first, while Dan. 10:2 ff. is an example of the second purpose of fasting. Daniel was in a burdened state of mind and spirit, but his attempts to understand the burdensome matter on his own had not been fruitful. He had plunged into a period of darkness, so he sought clarity and understanding from God. He prepared himself for this by fasting (v. 12). Daniel's plea was heard.

This account from the Book of Daniel is especially important as a teaching piece. Its appearance in a highly stylized book of apocalyptic writing should not lessen its ability to emphasize the practical importance of fasting as a way of preparing oneself for an encounter with God. The quest for knowledge is a particular concern in all apocalyptic writings; but it is also a practical necessity in situations where one needs particular guidance about how to handle oneself and face the issues of life with faith and wise courage.

## Jesus and fasting

By the time of Jesus, the practice of fasting had undergone extensive revision and was considered to be nothing more than a meritorious act characteristic of piety. Adjudging that a sufficient picture of first-century Jewish fasting is available in the Gospels, we must say that Jesus and His disciples stood conspicuously separate from the customary fasting practices of their time. The Gospels show no periods in which the disciples of Jesus fasted. The Temptation narratives given by Matthew and Luke indicate that Jesus disciplined himself by fasting (Matt. 4:2; Luke 4:2); but after those brief accounts, we are told nothing more about when Jesus may have engaged in this discipline. Mark 2:18-20 reports a controversy over the fact that the critics of Jesus never observed His disciples fasting. This controversy tells us many things:

1. The people who questioned Jesus' teachings and activities watched Him with conspicuous concern.

2. If Jesus' disciples did fast at His request, their fasting pattern (i.e., the days of fasting they observed) differed from that of the Pharisees, on the one hand, and the pattern of the disciples of John the Baptist, on the other.

3. Jesus replied to His critics at this point with His

parable of the children of the bridechamber (Mark 2:19-20; Matt. 9:14-15); the immediate point of this parable was that Jesus' presence forbade remorse among His disciples. The sorrow traditionally associated with fasting was absent at this time of joy.

4. Jesus did teach His disciples, however, that a time would come when fasting would be appropriate for them. His absence would stir them to the exercise of fasting: "The days will come, when the bridegroom is taken away from them, and then they will fast in that day" (Mark 2:20, RSV).

Jesus did not require His disciples to fast while He was with them; but it must be remembered that Jesus himself fasted before beginning His ministry, and He taught His disciples that certain occasions would call for the use of fasting. Jesus also gave them some teaching about how to fast in a creative, good-spirited way that is true to the purpose of a Christian fast. At a time when fasting was thought to be a meritorious act, Jesus centered their attention on the proper purpose and practice of fasting.

Matt. 6:16-18 makes it quite clear that fasting is to be done without pride or public notice. Jesus says nothing about the timing of the fast or the type of fast—whether it is to be restricted, as in Daniel's case (Dan. 10:2-3), or total, as in Jesus' own case while under testing in the wilderness (Luke 4:1 ff.). His words *and when you fast* might have been spoken with the Jews' national fast days in view; but they would also apply to private fasts an individual might undertake to seek divine help in personal crises or in the midst of personal concerns.[1]

Jesus gave few teachings on the subject of fasting; but the teachings He did give are quite clear and positive. For Jesus, fasting was a discipline of dignity and purpose. It was to be a hidden discipline, a secret deed before God. It was not meritorious (i.e., done to merit God's special favor).

*For Jesus, fasting was a discipline of dignity and purpose.*

In the parable of the Pharisee and the tax collector (Luke 18:9-14), Jesus illustrated the demand for an inner attitude to match the outward act in order to keep fasting from becoming an impractical and pietistic failure. Jesus indicated that the Pharisee of His parable was to be faulted because he considered himself righteous by what he practiced rather than by God's mercies to him. Jesus resisted the notion of depending on good works and merciful deeds; reliance upon these things had destroyed proper spiritual disciplines in the Jewish nation.

Jesus' teaching undercut the impractical controversies over fasting. His suggestive parable of the Pharisee and the tax collector is a good case in point. The Pharisee boasted that fasting was one of his weekly religious observances: "I fast twice a week" (Luke 18:12, RSV); presumably this was on Monday and Thursday—strategic timing, since those were the regular market days when the towns and cities would be filled with buyers and sellers, and special worship services were held in the synagogues. The Pharisee would have his reward, but not from God. Jesus forbade this sort of parading one's piety and urged the practice of religion without formalism and pride. He taught that fasting was to be a hidden discipline just as prayer was. "But when you fast, anoint your head and wash your face" (Matt. 6:17, RSV). Jesus sanctioned no disfiguring of the face and no exhibitionism by distinctive dress—practices of the Pharisees who did not use oil on their bodies during fast days because that oil might have touched Gentile hands, thereby bringing them defilement. The real defilement, Jesus indicated, is in the spirit that causes a person to exaggerate religious actions and call attention to those actions for self-honor. Because this intention is not holy, the entire self is defiled.

The teachings Jesus gave about fasting underscore that it is a hidden discipline, yet a definite way of dealing with the self before God.

## the early church and fasting

The Early Church practiced fasting, with important concerns and notable results. The Book of Acts shows us that the first Christian believers and church leaders made frequent use of this discipline in their private and corporate life. It does not appear that they considered fasting to be a mere carryover from their former Jewish ritual. Rather, the life situation of the Early Church compelled these Christians to see the creative importance of fasting.

We have seen that in the Old Testament period, fasting was used primarily within situations of sorrow, remorse, and repentance. But in the life of the Early Church, fasting was seen in a more creative context; it was used to express the worshiper's wholehearted response to God. Fasting became a way of sensitizing the human spirit to discern God's will. Acts 13:2-3 can be so understood: "While they were worshiping the Lord and fasting, the Holy Spirit said, 'Set apart for me Barnabas and Saul for the work to which I have called them.' Then after fasting and praying they laid their hands on them and sent them off" (RSV).

Here we see the church leaders fasting to obtain explicit guidance from God. Although the wording of the passage shows that the leaders were involved in fasting, this need not be taken to mean that *only* the leaders fasted. At any rate, the Christians who fasted did so with specific concern to be sensitive to what God would say to them. Fasting was a shared discipline among them, a corporate concern allied with group prayer. Acts 14:23 reports fasting in a similar context; the newly founded Christian congregations are commended to new leadership, and the service is marked by prayer and fasting.

The explicit bond between prayer and fasting—and between prayer, fasting, and corporate worship—shows us that fasting is a way of worship in the present Christian era. Fasting is not a law among many religious laws, but a living act that is avowedly ethical in dimension. Fasting is a discipline that leads to vision, understanding, and creative spiritual behavior. Fasting is a moral action that is spiritual in motivation and affirmative in tone (although self-denial is definitely involved in it). Fasting affirms our trust in God. It unites with prayer, strengthening that prayer. At times

*Fasting is a discipline that leads to vision, understanding, and creative spiritual behavior.*

we pray independently of fasting; but there are also times when circumstances require that fasting accompany our prayers. This was the case with Jesus as He fasted before God in the wilderness. It was also the case with the Early Church as its leaders faced difficult decisions and sought to know the mind of the Lord on the issues before them. This disciplined way of handling church concerns was carried over into the life of Christians in the postapostolic period, as the *Didache* (probably written after A.D. 62) certainly shows as it lifts fasting into view as an essential spiritual discipline of the Christian community, a way to active faith, a way to keep the self under subjection to the will of God. In the *Didache* we read, "Before the baptism, let the baptizer and the candidate for baptism fast, as well as any others that are able. Require the candidate to fast one or two days previously" (7:4).

Perhaps this prescription about fasting before baptism can be traced to a Jewish origin. However, we should recognize that the other forms of fasting practiced by Christians in the postapostolic era did not coincide with the fasting of the Jews. The *Didache* further instructed the Christians to make sure their fasts did not coincide with those of the hypocrites who fasted on Mondays and Thursdays (we presume this refers to the Pharisees); the Christians were urged to fast on Wednesdays and Fridays instead.

The subject of fasting received more elaborate treatment during the patristic period. The church fathers had many influences pressing upon their thought world: their indebtedness to Jewish ritual, their pilgrimages to the Holy Land, strife within the church, laity's plea for an emphasis on catechetical training, the ongoing moral and philosophical struggle between church and world, and the creation of specialized worship patterns in each major center of the church, to name but a few of the influences. Many documents describe that period of church history, and they are quite valuable.

All things considered, it should be said that the Fathers were strongly influenced by ascetic ideals, and they commended the ascetic life to their people, with heavy stress upon fasting as a Christian discipline. Fasting also became a form of church discipline, a penalty imposed in cases that did not warrant excommunication. Easter became the central festal day of the church during the patristic era. Christians' preparation for that day called for them to fast for a week; they were not to eat usual foods, not even bread or oil. Christians were told to take only gruel and water in the period of mourning from Good Friday to Easter (Easter being the time when their prepared catechumens were to be baptized). However, disputes arose over how many days Christians should observe as formal fast days; disputes also raged over what diet should be permitted during a fast. The Eastern church outstripped the West in developing strict rules for the fast diet and for establishing universal periods of fasting.

By the medieval period, these rules had become so elaborate that the fast was a mere religious form again, with Christians paying strict attention to days and diets rather than giving adequate concern for exercising the discipline as Jesus taught it. There is some historical evidence to suggest that fasting became a part of a ritual of penance in the medieval era, as it had been in Old Testament times; the church apparently lost the creative understanding of fasting that the Early Church knew and practiced in the Book of Acts. Ivo of Chartres, for example, alluded to almsgiving, prayer, and fasting as three kinds of spiritual medicine in his sermon on the Lord's Prayer. He urged almsgiving "to cleanse the crimes which take place outside the body, granting profit to others where one has done harm; prayer, to cure the diseases of the soul; and fasting—because as the willing flesh has brought us fault, so, when afflicted, it ought to lead back to pardon."[2] By the medieval era there were so many teachings about the purpose and methods of fasting that entire systems of doctrine were being based on this discipline, and it was embellished with speculative ideas. The New Testament dimension of the discipline had been lost.

## some modern purposes of fasting

In our own time we have seen fasting used for still other reasons than religious ones. Some physicians now recommend fasting as a way to solve the problem of being overweight. Here it is a case of disciplined diet for the sake of the body, relief from overeating, and relief for an overworked digestive system; so this kind of fast may be termed a *relief fast*. Mahatma Gandhi was known to use fasting in this way, as a discipline of self-restraint and as a means of cultivating a tempered body. The ancient note of asceticism rings clear in Gandhi's statement that one should not eat to please the palate but to keep the body going. Gandhi confessed that he began fasting out of concern for a sound body. In later life he said that he was still accustomed to fasting occasionally for health reasons.

But Gandhi came to see another dimension of this discipline: It could be practiced as a coercive action to bring about moral and political change. This may be called a *coercive fast.* This kind of fast, publicly announced and publicly oriented, calls attention to an evil in society that should be corrected. Gandhi undertook this method of self-penance to sting the conscience of others into right action; many of Gandhi's fasts fall into this category. E. Stanley Jones recalled a conversation with Gandhi during which the Indian leader explained the rationale of such a fast. The conversation took place in the Yeravda Jail, where Gandhi was being held by British officials. Jones asked, "Isn't your fasting a species of coercion?"

*Fasting can be practiced as a coercive action to bring about moral and political change.*

Gandhi's answer was immediate and deliberate: "Yes, the same kind of coercion which Jesus exercises upon you from the Cross."

Jones pondered that for a long while. "It was so obviously true," he later commented, "that I am silent again every time I think of it. He was profoundly right. The years have clarified it."[3]

The fastings of the Mahatma were calculated to be a public witness to moral issues involving the public. The potency of this kind of moral appeal can be seen in the following instance from Gandhi's life as a political leader. During 1932 the British offered India a constitution that was designed to grant electoral power to Hindus, Muslims, and the Untouchables—but the Untouchables were to vote separately. Gandhi opposed the proposed constitution on both political and religious grounds. He believed the plan would further divide the people, making their already separate life more deeply entrenched. Yet public reaction did not support Gandhi's point of view; many Indian leaders considered this a minor issue. When Gandhi saw that the public was not as he urged it to be, he made the critical decision: If the British government forced the creation of a separate electorate for the Untouchables, he would fast unto death. It was his way of publicly protesting a moral issue that he believed to be crucial.

Ramsay MacDonald, British minister of the government, was bewildered by Gandhi's announced plan. Nehru was also displeased with Gandhi, thinking that his fast was unwise and drew unnecessary attention to the issue of the Untouchables. But Gandhi was determined. His fast was not pretentious. The days passed as Gandhi refused the meals that were brought to his jail cell. Finally, the prison officials announced that Gandhi was so feeble that his condition was dangerously low; death could be expected at any time. Gandhi was forcing an ultimatum by his decisive deed. He wanted to sting the Hindu conscience into action against a proposal that was not in the best interests of the nation as a whole. He was fasting to arouse public emotions on a point of moral concern. The fast was a frank public appeal. In so fasting, Gandhi made each Hindu personally responsible for his life—and death—for if he died, every apathetic Hindu would be his murderer! Suffice it to say that the Indian people rushed into action at the last moment and resisted the proposed constitution. Gandhi lived, but his physical wounds from the fast were meaningfully borne for the rest of his life, along with his redemptive concern. His deed had saved the nation.

Impressed by Gandhi's example and the change it wrought, Martin Luther King Jr. seriously considered whether he should undertake a "fast unto death" until black Americans would forswear all violence in their struggle for equal civil rights and until all black leaders, both moderate and militant, would unite in a strictly nonviolent program for social change. King was deeply disturbed and depressed by black disunity during the last months of his life. Such a fast would have been coercive, with the intent to sting the conscience of every black American into voluntary nonviolence as the most practical and moral course to effect social change. But King did not live to attempt the deed.

## fasting for spiritual resourcefulness

Our discussion of fasting has taken us through many centuries of religious life and along at least four major areas of applied concern. We have noted that fasting has been

1. a discipline of penitence and remorse
2. a way of spiritual resourcefulness
3. a means of physical relief, and
4. a protest measure to effect social results

In keeping with our concern to understand fasting in the light of the life of Jesus and the Early Church, let us return to a consideration of the use of fasting as a discipline for spiritual resourcefulness.

Fasting is important in Christian experience because it deepens within the whole self a sense of one's dependence upon the strength of God. Fasting is more than an act of abstinence. It is an affirmative act; it is a way of waiting on God; it is an act of surrender. Fasting tends to induce within us an awareness of the spiritual dimension of life. Fasting is not a renunciation of life; it is a means by which new life is released within us. Fasting is not done to denigrate the flesh or subject it to torture as if it were an unworthy part of the self. Every part of the self is essential; no part is alien. Fasting helps us to grapple directly with any resistance from troublesome aspects of the self—the body, for instance, making us come to terms with such pressuring concerns by a spirit of discipline and trust.

Fasting expands the consciousness, permitting us to learn from wider dimensions of life as God knows and wills it for us. Certain areas of understanding and experience lie beyond our usual awareness; fasting is a calculated attempt to release ourselves into a sensitive awareness of those areas. Fasting sensitizes. Fasting strengthens. Fasting confirms a positive openness to God. Fasting allows a kind of self-death and resurrection.

Granted, the inward dynamics of the act can be discussed in terms of psychology. The validity of the act can be defended in terms of biblical tradition. But the spiritual value of the act can be understood only in terms of personal experience.

# notes

1. Several passages in the Psalms reflect individual fasts undertaken quite apart from national fast days. I would so consider Psalm 35:13 and 69:10, where the context suggests a personal concern for divine help in one person's time of crisis.

2. Ivo of Chartres, *Early Christian Theology,* trans. and ed. by George E. McCracken and Allen Cabaniss (London: SCM Press Ltd., n.d.), 322-23.

3. E. Stanley Jones, *Mahatma Gandhi: An Interpretation* (Nashville: Abingdon, 1948), 110.

James Earl Massey is dean emeritus and distinguished professor-at-large at Anderson University School of theology in Anderson, Indiana. This chapter is reprinted with permission from Dr. Massey's book *Spiritual Disciplines* (Grand Rapids: Zondervan Corporation, 1985), 53-67.

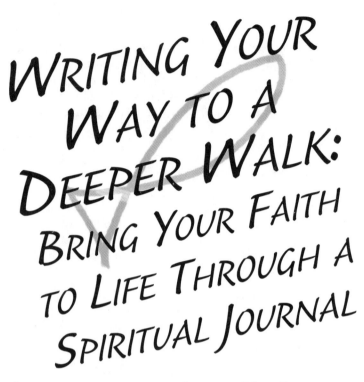

# Writing Your Way to a Deeper Walk: Bring Your Faith to Life Through a Spiritual Journal

## jeanette gardner littleton

**Maybe I'm a packrat,** but in a file cabinet in our garage are two big gray file drawers filled with notebooks. Some of them have survived about 30 years. Their covers are somewhat battered, and their pages certainly aren't pristine. They've moved with me to six different homes over these past three decades. And they'll probably age quite a bit more before I finally give in to getting rid of them.

The notebooks vary. Some have a plastic coating with raised designs of sunbonneted girls, and cutesy sayings like "Please be patient, God's not finished with me yet." Some are plain spiral-bound notebooks. Many others are stenographers' notebooks. But they're all filled with the ponderings, prayers, and insights of my spiritual life through the years.

I think I first started filling notebooks when I was about 15 years old. I worked many weeks of my summers in the snack shop of a Christian teen camp. Most of my friends worked in the kitchen and had different break times, so I was often on my own during free times. I would walk the quiet, cool horse trails through the camp's woods. We heard morning and evening messages from some of the best youth speakers of the '70s, and I steadily read my Bible every day. So sometimes, my soul just seemed too full to hold all of my questions and thoughts. I started taking a notebook and pen with me on my nature walks and would stop here and there to put the overflow on paper.

Through the years, keeping spiritual journals has been an invaluable tool to my spiritual walk, and it's a practice you might enjoy too.

## benefits of a spiritual journal

Just as writing in a standard journal can help us keep track of our thoughts and experiences in life, a spiritual journal can help us keep track of our walk with Christ.

Any time we write out our thoughts, the act of writing helps us organize our thoughts, work through them, and solidify them. Writing about our spiritual ponderings and questions helps our faith gel. Writing can take us to a deeper level of thinking about a matter, or open our eyes to new ideas.

Another great reason to keep a spiritual journal is to show us the journeys we've traveled in our faith. For instance, I can look back through my journals and see how my faith progressed. I can see what issues and insights were important to me at certain stages in my life.

And as we look through and see the journeys we've taken in our faith, we see how much God has taught us, how much we've grown, and how God has worked in our lives. This gives us hope, encouragement, and sometimes even a sort of "déjà vu" guidance for the spiritual issues we're dealing with today.

Keeping a spiritual journal can also just help our whole spiritual awareness. As we write about the spiritual aspect of our lives, we become more aware of our spiritual journeys and pay more attention to God's voice and acts. We'll better see how God's Word applies to our lives and will probably begin praying more during the day.

Keeping a spiritual journal also helps us with the "act" of "doing daily devotions." It helps build our relationship with God. As you write about that relationship and spiritual growth process, you'll find you're paying more attention to what you read and pray. Instead of just being a "duty" or "discipline," your devotional time will start coming to life and being an exciting process—something you can't wait to do!

## a tool to fit your needs

Start with a notebook and a pen you find easy to write with. Keep your journal nearby each day as you read the Bible and pray. As God brings thoughts to your mind during your time with Him, write them in your journal.

You can go as simple or as organized as you like. You might want to start simply, with just a notebook. As time passes, you might realize you'd really like a notebook with different sections so you can have different focuses (prayer, Bible study, spiritual questions, ponderings, etc.) or different types of journaling (prayers, poems, Bible stories, devotions, artwork, etc.).

Your spiritual journal is something that may adapt or change as you adapt or change. The kinds of entries you put in your journal today might not be what you want to do in the future. And that's OK. It's a tool to help *you*. It needs to help you keep your spiritual life fresh.

*Your spiritual journal is something that may adapt or change as you adapt or change.*

Get as creative as you like in your spiritual journal. And at the same time, don't worry about how polished your writing is. This is just for you. It's a book about you and God, for you.

You might keep your journal handy to write in once a day. Or perhaps it will become such a part of your life that you'll want to carry it with you and jot notes throughout the day. Either way is OK—or anything in between.

## ideas for what you might want to include

You can include many things in your spiritual journal, but here are some ideas to help you get started. Pick and choose the ones you'd like to try. You might even pick out one different thing to try for each day. Do whatever works (and makes it fun) for you!

- Bible study notes. As you sit down with your Bible for a devotional time, make sure your spiritual journal is handy. Take notes about what you read in the Bible. List any observations, insights, or questions. Or create a summary of the passage you've read to help you remember it.

- Verses for memorization. You can keep a list of verses you're working on putting in your heart and mind, or that you'd like to memorize. In my early years, I found that repeatedly writing verses helped me memorize them, so some of my journals are filled with scriptures written over and over (or written as my own personal review test later).

- Prayers. If you ever feel your prayers aren't getting through to God, you may want to write them out.

- Prayer requests. This is a great place to keep track of personal and intercessory needs. Date a prayer request as you list it, and leave room for a date and comment when you see God answer your prayer. In one Sunday School class I taught, we kept a prayer journal for the class of teen girls. How excited they were to actually be able to track the thought that God answered prayers. This is a wonderful source of encouragement in our spiritual lives—to actually be able to look back and see how and when God answered specific prayers. This is also a great idea for a family to do.

- Devotionals. Shortly after I became a Christian 30 years ago, I started reading devotional books and magazines. With that writing style in mind, I started writing down my own devotional thoughts in my spiritual journals. Soon my goal was to write a devotional every day from the scriptures I read. That helped me really concentrate until God gave me a nugget to chew on.
- Characters of the Bible. At another point in my spiritual walk, I focused on the people I read about. My spiritual journal included written sketches of them and what I imagined they felt in the different situations.
- Poetry. Does your soul wax poetic when you contemplate your walk with Christ? This is a great place to keep those poems and songs your soul sings out.
- Artwork. If you're an artist, draw scenes or the visuals that the scripture brings to your mind. (If you're an artist, draw pictures of scenes you are reading about!)
- Fact lists. Sometimes I've created timelines of people or events I find in my Bible reading. Making a family tree while reading genealogies and noting where else these people pop up in Scripture can be eye-opening!
- Focus on the senses. Sometimes I've used my senses to imagine the scenes—for instance, listing what it might have smelled like, looked like, sounded like, and even tasted like when the paralytic was lowered through the roof.
- Application. As you read in God's Word, write

down how these verses apply to you personally and how you can better live out the verses in your life. Perhaps you can keep a list of specific goals. For instance, if you're reading about Rom. 12:21: "Do not be overcome by evil, but overcome evil with good," list practical ways you can follow this scripture in your life.

- Be a storyteller. Tell a scripture story in your own words. You may want to give it a twist, like the people who tell the story of the prodigal son, primarily using words that start with the letter *p*—a real tongue twister to listen to!

- Modernize the stories. Similar to telling the story, modernize it for children, teens, or other adults. Write the story in today's lingo, and create the settings as if Jesus were using today's illustrations.

- Dramas. Speaking of settings, try to create skits and dramas based in the scripture you read. For instance, once as I read about Jesus, I started thinking of His role as a single man. I wondered if He was often nagged by His relatives to get married, and how they viewed that consecration to God. I created a skit with a man lamenting to a friend about his single nephew, who turned out to be Jesus. It was a fun skit to write, and a drama troupe later picked it up. Another time I wrote a skit about the feeding of the 5,000—from the paper bag's perspective. Have fun with it!

- Favorite quotes. Are you a person who likes quotes? In your journal, you might want to write your favorite quotes (or poems or songs) that are authored by other people. Be sure to include the author's name and maybe even the source where you found the quote in case you ever need to refer to it.

- Sermon notes. You can either tote your spiritual journal with you to church and pull it out when you listen to your favorite preachers on the radio or TV, or you can put the "best of" the notes in your spiritual journal.

- Lists of people. In his spiritual journaling, my husband, Mark, has kept lists of people he wants to lead to Christ. This prompts him to pray for these people and to look for ways to minister to them. If you're sometimes forgetful about people, as I am, it might be helpful to make notes about the people too—facts you don't want to forget, like where they work or interests they mention.

- Spiritual reaction. In your journal, you might want to keep tack of current events—and your valuation of them in the light of God's Word or your relationship with God.

- Questions. If you could talk to God face-to-face, what would you ask Him? What are the questions—about verses, or about life—that come to your mind as you read the Scriptures? What are the questions you have about God, the holy life, and being a Christian in a non-Christian world? Write them down in your journal.

- Family facts. You might want a section in your spiritual journal to keep track of your kids' spiritual growth. This might be a place to write down when your six-year-old has come to a new step in faith, or your kids' interpretations of Scripture verses. Or you could recount a spiritually based conversation you had with one of your kids. This will help your children when they're older and want to build their own spiritual heritage.

- Daily happenings. List things in your day that had an impact on your spiritual life. For instance, I was involved in a meeting one day with a person I had endured a conflict with and dreaded facing. God spoke to me about the situation with thoughts that will be good to remember later.

- Reviews of cultural things from a spiritual standpoint. As you watch videos, read books, or listen to CDs, keep the spiritual perspective in mind (how does the message of the medium match up with Scripture and the mind that God wants us to have?). Write down your analysis. You could also do reviews or summaries of Christian books and CDs you've read and listened to.

- Spiritual goals list. Just as many of us have lists to help us accomplish goals in our homelife or work, it could be beneficial to keep a list of things you'd like to do in your spiritual life—goals you'd like to accomplish, books you'd like to read, and so forth. That helps give us direction and helps us actually achieve some of those desires.

- Milestones. While you're writing your current spiritual history in your journal, you can also use your journal as a place to recount your past spiritual history. Write down what you remember about accepting Christ, or understanding the Holy Spirit's role in your life. Jot down what made you start reading your Bible. Mention special events in your spiritual walk, like times God clearly spoke to you or guided you. After all, the Old Testament is full of instances where God's people built an altar or an "Ebenezer" or even just a pile of stones as a physical reminder of a spiritual victory in their lives.

- Word studies. When you find a verse that has a word that intrigues you, or piques your curiosity, use your dictionary, Bible encyclopedias, and various versions of the Bible to look at words in verses from a different angle.

- Comparative scripture studies. Compare scriptures in different versions. Write them down in your spiritual journal, along with how you think different versions emphasize different points.

- Memories. Similar to writing about your milestones, write about memories, using as much description as possible. One day I wrote about the lazy summer Sunday evenings I loved so much in Dundee Hills Church of the Nazarene. I described how the sanctuary looked and sounded and what I felt and saw through my young eyes when people stood up and testified.

- Spiritual mission statement. Most corporations, organizations, and even homes have a mission statement. What's your personal, spiritual mission statement?

- Missionary minutes. Keep track of your favorite missionaries or ministries. Write notes about their work. You can even jot how God is calling you to pray for them.

- Contemplations. A spiritual journal is a great place to keep your disjointed thoughts and con-

templations—especially those you can't really
articulate. Never worry that your thoughts are
not smooth enough to write them in your journal
—write them anyway. God may use your act of
writing to make sense of them.

- "Where is God in my life today?" You can have a
  section with this title, where you keep an honest,
  ongoing analysis of your relationship with God.
- Teaching moments. Keep track of verses and
  ideas that you can use to teach unsaved friends
  about God. Note verses and scriptural thoughts
  God brings to your mind that you can pass along
  to your kids, Sunday School class, or anyone else
  within your scope of influence.

## variations on a theme

Although writing our thoughts on paper is great,
you may be one of those people for whom the thought
of actually writing makes you very tired. Are you too
computer-oriented for a good old-fashioned journal
(or too afraid you'll end up with packed filing drawers
like mine!). Create files on your computer for your
spiritual journal. For instance, keep one large docu-
ment in which you type each day's thoughts. Or keep a
separate folder for each day. You can have a folder for
your prayer journal and a separate folder for your
scripture journal—or combine the two.

If you're concerned about privacy, you can put a
password protection on your computer files contain-
ing the journal. Or find a good location where you can
keep your notebook journal that will be a personal,
private place.

If you're keeping a general journal, at some stage, whether on paper or on the computer, you may want to organize your thoughts into different categories for easy reference. File folders (on the computer and the standard paper ones) can help you organize categories. Follow whatever system works best for you! But if you take your journal out of a chronological order, still date every entry. Later reading what happened in your life or what God taught you on a certain date may help you see God at work in a certain way. And though we think we'll never forget when certain events happen, we often do. Make it easy on your memory and jot dates.

*Later reading what happened in your life or what God taught you on a certain date may help you see God at work in a certain way.*

You might soon catch yourself jotting notes down for your spiritual journal at times when you don't have your spiritual journal with you. Don't let the fact that you don't have your journal with you keep you from writing. If you're keeping an actual paper journal, you can staple, glue, or tape any papers filled with these thoughts to your journal pages. Or choose a notebook with pockets in it for your spiritual journal. If your journal is on the computer, simply type in the other entries from different times in the day.

Three-hole binders might be another option if you like to write throughout the day. Put your daily entries in your binder each night. If you use a Day-Timer or other personal organizer, you might want to keep some blank pages in a section of your organizer and file them when filled. Likewise, if you use a Palm Pilot, you might want to keep a folder on it for journaling, and download that to your computer files every night or two.

But again, don't be afraid to start simple and vary your journaling routine and needs as you go along.

As you seek a way to become closer to God's heart, start the habit of keeping a spiritual journal. You'll love the results in your life!

Jeanette Gardner Littleton is a freelance writer and editor from Kansas City. This chapter is an expansion of an article first published in *Holiness Today*, January 2004.

# Finding My Places of Service

## janine tartaglia-metcalf

**Concerned friends told Los Angeles**
Mission worker Rich Verbal it couldn't be done—it shouldn't be done. Taking a group of homeless men from skid row on a camping trip to the mountains was beyond the call of duty, even dangerous. How would this motley troop fare in the wilderness? How would they get along with each other?

Rich wasn't sure. All he knew was that the idea was born in prayer and that if God wanted him to follow through, He would provide the grace and supplies to do it. As Rich saw it, the benefits of such a journey far outweighed the barriers. Camping under the stars would show the former gang members that there was more to the sky than smog, more to the earth's floor than concrete, and more to the animal kingdom than rats and pigeons. With faith, borrowed tents, and fishing poles, he took the van load of young men from six different cultures on a four-day adventure.

The results were phenomenal. Cultural differences disappeared as the men fished, rode bikes, sang, and testified around the campfire. Ray, an ex-convict who was forced to grow up quickly on the streets, summed up the group's appreciation: "For the first time ever, I was able to release the child bottled up inside of me."

That release came as the result of their leader's obedience. Rich wasn't a psychologist or an ordained elder, just a willing servant with a deep love for God and a genuine concern for his homeless brothers.

Holy service evolves from this kind of surrendered lifestyle. When our motives are pure and our hearts are filled with Christlike love, we can impact our homes, churches, neighborhoods, workplaces, and world. In this chapter we will examine service opportunities awaiting us when we offer up all we have and do for God's glory.

> **Let us go forth, 'tis Christ commands,**
> **let us make haste away.**
> **We offer to Christ our heart and hands,**
> **we work for Christ today.**
> —Charles Wesley

The Bible makes it clear that service is not a means of salvation but the natural product of our holy hearts. And as we grow in Christ, there is a natural "rhythm or flow from inspiration to incarnation, from prayer to participation, from contemplation to action."[1]

William Barclay contends: "It is a fact that every time a man feels a noble impulse without taking action, he becomes less likely ever to take action. In a sense it is true to say that a man has no right to feel sympathy unless he at least tries to put that sympathy into action."[2]

To help fulfill our call to holy service, God has equipped us with one or more spiritual gifts. These are unique abilities the Holy Spirit gives us after our conversion that enable us to build up and encourage others. The great majority of gifts are mentioned in Rom. 12:6-8; 1 Cor. 12:4-11; and Eph. 4:11. Every believer has at least one of these gifts and will be held accountable to use it.

If you have any doubt, take another look at Jesus' parable of the talents. He described three stewards who received different quantities of capital. Their responsibility was to use their resource to make more money. Two of the three succeeded and doubled their money. When the day of accounting came, each was called "good and faithful servant" (Matt. 25:21, 23). The other steward failed to recognize the potential of the resource he had. He did nothing with his capital and was judged a "wicked, lazy servant" (v. 26; see vv. 14-30).

From this story we learn that whatever resources we have received from God cannot be hidden but must be used to accomplish the Master's purpose. Many Christians are accomplishing God's purpose without being able to describe their specific gifts. There is biblical ground, however, for knowing and developing these gifts. Paul urges, "Now about spiritual gifts, brothers, I do not want you to be ignorant" (1 Cor. 12:1). One reason we should not be ignorant is that understanding and using our gifts will help the church to function. When "each separate part works as it should, the whole body grows" (Eph. 4:16, TEV).

The church body will grow, however, only as each part (Christian) relies on the Holy Spirit for gifting and direction. We cannot casually browse through gifts like a shopping list and pick whichever one sounds good. Nor are we free to choose no gift and opt out of Christian service. Without self-giving service, all other spiritual formation activities are reduced to mere shadowboxing.

## service as a spiritual discipline in the home

The first place we should exercise our gifts to serve is in our home with those who are closest to us. Richard Foster contends, "The dictum for the household should be 'Let each of you look not only to his own interests, but also to the interests of others' (Phil. 2:4, RSV). Freely and graciously the members of the family [should] make allowance for each other."[3]

Before racing out to fulfill their call as holy servants in the world, husbands and wives should first express God's love to each other. They need to

*Serve each other permission* to discuss misunderstandings, reveal hurt feelings, air frustrations, and ask difficult questions.

*Serve each other freedom* to make and recover from mistakes.

*Serve each other understanding* not only to tolerate

but to celebrate the differences in their character and personality traits. When we quit passing moral judgment and learn more about our separate temperaments, we open the door for workable compromise.

*Serve each other encouragement* to be all God wants us to be and do what God calls us to do. Men should be encouraged to break out of the macho, independent mold shaped by society and place their lives under God's control. At the same time, women need encouragement to develop inner security that comes from pleasing God. A husband's openness and input can help his wife overcome cultural pressures either to stay home or to venture into the marketplace. Couples should also

*Serve each other time.* Solid relationships require regular breaks built into our busy schedules for "dates" to enjoy each other's company. Finally, it is essential for a husband and wife to

*Serve each other authentic love.* First, love needs to be offered verbally. It is important to tell each other regularly, "I love you." We need to back up our words with affectionate action. Whatever is said and done in love will build a mate's self-esteem and have a powerful impact on the entire family.

Raising children in a healthy, secure home requires years of sacrificial service. Henri Nouwen reminds us:

> Children are not properties to own and rule over, but gifts to cherish and care for. Our children are our most important guests, who enter into our home, ask for careful attention, stay for a while and then leave to follow their own way. . . . What

parents can offer is a home, a place that is receptive but also has the safe boundaries within which their children can discover what is helpful and what is harmful. There their children can ask questions without fear and can experiment with life without taking the risk of rejection.[4]

Parents need to serve their children with fervent prayers to protect them, wisdom to guide them, fair discipline to train them, and opportunities to instill responsibility. Assigned chores let children know they are contributing members of the family.

> **There should be less talk; a preaching point**
> **is not a meeting point. What do you do then?**
> **Take a broom and clean someone's house.**
> **That says enough.**
> —Mother Teresa of Calcutta

The foremost concern in raising children should be to introduce them to a dynamic relationship with Jesus. Neill Hamilton claims this often is not the case: "I am afraid that most parish parents are content with their parenting if their children move smoothly to acquire the manners and education necessary for upward mobility. Parents are better at equipping their children to grow up achievers than they are at equipping them to grow up Christian."[5]

So much of what children feel about God and the Church is developed by watching their parents. I had a roommate, for instance, who grew up in a home where hurting, lonely people were welcomed and housed for as long as they needed. Throughout her high school years Dana watched her parents offer hospitality to teenagers and young adults craving love and stability. This invaluable service influenced Dana's Christian walk. Following her parent's example, she frequently turned our apartment into a hospice for new believers who needed love and nurturing.

Singles, too, are called to love and serve those God has placed in their lives, especially friends and housemates. Simple expressions of care, such as praying for each other, listening to each other's experiences, fulfilling household chores, paying bills on time, and respecting each other's possessions and privacy, create an atmosphere of hospitality.

Unbelievers may be able to serve each other with the same consideration, but it takes a holy life to consistently want to serve others. Our surrender coupled with God's grace can transform a home into a haven of safety where all are affirmed and encouraged to grow in Christ.

## service as a spiritual discipline in the church

The church committed to holy service is made up of Christians who have an intense love and feeling of responsibility for each other. Believers are bonded by

### 1. A Call to Community

Christians should have a compelling desire to give themselves away for the common good. Charles R. Swindoll claims this corporate identity in Christ turns believers from "marbles" to "grapes." "Every congregation . . . can choose to be a bag of marbles, single units that don't affect each other except in collision. Or . . . a bag of grapes. The juices begin to mingle, and there is no way to extricate yourselves if you tried. Each is a part of all. Part of the fragrance . . . [and] sometimes we 'grapes' really bleed and hurt."[6]

The joy of being a part of a church with a serving heart is that no one bleeds and hurts alone. Regardless of our trials or triumphs, someone will come alongside and share the experience with us.

Ask Miriam. She was 76 years old when she asked Christ into her heart. Her first Christmas as a child of the King, however, almost changed her mind. First, she caught a nasty cold. Second, she was fired from her job. Then her dogs broke down the fence in her front yard at about the same time her wall heater died. As she shivered in her frigid little house, Miriam heard several gunshots. Running outside, she found one of her dogs lying dead on the front lawn. The other dog was injured.

Miriam was devastated and cried out, "What's with You, God? Don't You love me anymore?" She screamed so loud that she almost didn't hear the phone ring. The call was from one of her new friends from church who felt led by God to phone Miriam "to see if everything was all right." Miriam was stunned. How did her friend know she needed help?

The friend listened and immediately came over with firewood to heat Miriam's house and an extra hand to take the wounded dog to the veterinarian. The next day an electrician from the church came to repair her heater while a handyman from the church put up the front yard fence. A few days later a Sunday School class took up an offering to help Miriam pay her bills. They came to her door singing carols, bearing a big basket of food and a decorated Christmas tree, complete with lights and ornaments. "God loves you, Miriam," one of the carolers exclaimed.

"I know," she admitted. "I now really know."

The spontaneous care from other believers prompted Miriam to stay in the church and become involved in the pantry ministry for the homeless.

## 2. A Call to Responsibility

If holiness is to be expressed through good works, then the church is called to equip, motivate, and send *all* believers into service. Hear the rally cry of pastor and lay ministry leader James Garlow: "Contrary to popular opinion Christianity is not a spectator sport. Every believer is a minister! Everyone is involved."[7]

This involvement was extensively promoted by John Wesley, who trained 653 lay preachers during his half century of active ministry. The early Methodist system gave ample room for laypersons to serve as class leaders, band leaders, stewards, visitors of the sick, schoolmasters, and housekeepers.

Thomas Gillespie contends this sweeping lay revolution will continue today, but "only if the 'nonclergy' are willing to move up, if the 'clergy' are willing to move over, and if all God's people are willing to move out."[8]

As we minister together not only as servants but as true friends of Jesus and each other, we can fulfill Paul's command to "do good to all people, especially to those who belong to the family of believers" (Gal. 6:10).

At one church I attended, members heeded the

commission to "carry each other's burdens" (Gal. 6:2) in a variety of ways. Teens visited shut-ins. Shut-ins wrote encouragement cards to teens. Young couples renovated the homes of members in financial trouble. Older couples "adopted" young families by frequently contacting them and interceding for them. Mechanics assisted widows with car problems. Accountants counseled single parents surviving on limited incomes. And prayer groups of all ages regularly met to lift the church's praises and petitions to the throne. The call to holy servants extends beyond where we live and where we worship to where we work. When Christians walk on the job they should be thinking about more than making money, impressing the boss, or surviving until the weekend. Regardless of where we work, ultimately we are to serve Christ and the people for whom He died.

Paul makes it clear that "whatever you do, work at it with all your heart, as working for the Lord, not for men, since you know that you will receive an inheritance from the Lord as a reward. It is the Lord Christ you are serving" (Col. 3:23-24). In other words, our ultimate boss is Jesus.

The songs of our spiritual ancestors, the early Wesleyans, should be ours. This song was titled "On Their Going to Work."

> *Let us go forth, 'tis Christ commands,*
> *Let us make haste away.*
> *We offer to Christ our hearts and hands,*
> *We work for Christ today.*[9]
> —Charles Wesley

## service as a spiritual discipline in the world

The more God's servants heed His upward call to holiness, the more concerned and involved we must be with His idolatrous world. Our journey is not to retreat to a stained-glass ghetto to wait patiently and passively for the consummation of the Kingdom. Rather we must live and work for the sake of the Kingdom now. We are partners with Christ to promote His righteousness and justice throughout creation. Our global mission is threefold,

1. *Witnessing the Gospel:* We are called to preach and model the Good News to all people.

2. *Charity:* We are called to offer relief to the needy and oppressed.

3. *Social Action:* We are called to hold social structures accountable to Kingdom principles.

### 1. Servants Are Called to Witness for the Gospel

Holy servants are called to live and proclaim the gospel so as to win people to a personal faith in Jesus Christ. It is not enough to introduce them to Jesus; we must disciple them to submit their lives to His grace, Lordship, and mission.

Often the toughest mission field is witnessing to those we know and love the most. I shared my frustrations with former Nazarene General Superintendent Dr. Edward Lawlor one day. He advised me to find a pen and paper to record his answer. When I returned, he offered three ways to witness to my lost loved ones. "Number one: kindness and understanding. Number two: kindness and understanding. Number three:

kindness and understanding." His advice reshaped my approach to sharing Christ with others.

We also need to be involved in the church's corporate mission to proclaim Christ to our neighboring community and world. I am reminded of the redemptive work by several of my friends who are following in the footsteps of John Wesley.

- Mulham sponsors a neighborhood weekly Bible study that has attracted a growing number of Jordanian believers and nonbelievers near his home.
- Debbie consistently invites unsaved friends to church. Her ministry has helped win more than 15 people to Christ in the last two years.
- Mary has struggled with cancer for years. Still, between chemo treatments, she offers Bibles and blankets to families in Tijuana.
- Chuck is a financial advisor who enjoys interaction with people of different cultures on Work and Witness projects.
- John heads up a young couples' missionary chapter that is devoted to assisting home mission churches all over Southern California.

## 2. Servants Are Called to Aid the Poor

Throughout the Bible we see God taking special interest in the needy and inviting us to do the same. John F. Alexander observes, "The fatherless, widows, and foreigners each have about forty verses that command justice for them. God wants to make it very clear that in a special sense He is the protector of these weak ones. Strangers are to be treated nearly the same as Jews, and woe to people who take advantage of orphans or widows."[10] Prov. 14:31 reminds us: "He who oppresses the poor shows contempt for their Maker." At the same time, "He who is kind to the poor lends to the LORD" (19:17).

The best way to help the poor is to identify with them. That's what Jesus did. Paul tells us that "though he was rich, yet for your sakes he became poor" (2 Cor. 8:9). He was born in a lowly stable. His parents were too poor to bring the normal offering for purification (Luke 2:24). During His public ministry He didn't have a home of His own (Matt. 8:20). He even sent out His disciples in poverty (Luke 9:3; 10:4).

So what does this mean to you and me? It means that we are to follow Christ's example by choosing to be with the poor. May we listen to them, learn from them, and express Christlike mercy to them.

John Wesley contended that there was no split between personal salvation and social engagement. He and his reformers worked tirelessly for the spiritual and material welfare of those victimized by industrialization. Wesley spread scriptural holiness and reformed the nation by establishing social services, such as orphanages, poorhouses, food and clothes pantries, a free medical clinic, a "lying in" hospital for unwed mothers, and boarding schools for children otherwise destined for work in the sweatshops and mines.

**Let us not grow weary in well-doing,
for in due season we shall reap, if we do not lose
heart. So then . . . let us do good to all men.**
—Gal. 6:9, RSV

On top of that, Wesley urged Christians to give away all but "the plain necessaries of life—that is plain, wholesome food, clean clothes and enough to carry on one's business."[11] He lived what he preached. Sales of his books often earned him £1,400 annually, but he spent only £30 pounds on himself. The rest he gave away. He always wore inexpensive clothes and dined on simple food.[12]

Regardless of our incomes, *all* believers are called to conform spending and working habits with a sensitivity to the needs of others. We should stop buying frivolous things in order to generously give more to God's causes. Parents should model biblical stewardship to their children. Richard Foster writes, "Neither Jesus nor any of the apostles confined giving to the tithe—they went beyond it. In all their teachings, generosity and sacrifice loom large. This is true whether we are looking at the poor widow giving her mite or Barnabas giving a parcel of land to the early church."[13]

### 3. Servants Are Called to Social Action

As holy servants we are called to promote God's peace in a world infected by greed, permissiveness, and selfishness. With Jesus as our model and the Spirit as our enabler—

*We can confront injustice.* We should commend our government, schools, and health organizations whenever they act to preserve biblical standards. We should support leaders or assume leadership ourselves to initiate change for the public good. It is our right and responsibility to stand up for the rights of the unborn, the elderly, the mentally retarded, and others who are unable to fend for themselves. We can do this through prayer, vigorous nonviolent demonstration, and personal intervention into the lives of suffering people. May we as individuals and together as the Body of Christ *intentionally* seek those shunned by society to offer them God's healing grace and hope.

Some servants may feel led to expose injustice by taking part in civil disobedience. Before we challenge civil authority, however, Christians must make sure they are walking in the authority, power, and love of the Holy Spirit.

*We can confront immorality.* Sin has distorted our world's view of sexuality. May we as God's servants exemplify good morals and speak out against pornography and promiscuous behavior so often promoted by the media. Parents need to teach and model for their children what the Bible says about sexuality and proper relationships.

We also need to hold the media accountable for its publications and programming that so often condone immoral behavior. We should voice our displeasure by writing well-researched, concise letters to publishers, television producers, and sponsors. Our opinions can make a difference.

*And we can confront pollution.* It's time to become better stewards of God's creation. Our homes and churches should explore creative ways to conserve more and consume less. Christ's servants should take the lead in recycling to cut down waste. We should also help to clean up our communities for future generations.

Before moving on, stop and think about your spiritual journey as God's servant. Recall the people and needs He has placed on your path and your response to them. While heeding the upward call, have you received and imparted God's grace to your family, to your church, to friends at work, neighbors across the street, and strangers you've met? Have you used the spiritual gifts, possessions, and personality God has given you to improve the quality of life around you? Are you consumed by a passion to *be* good news as well as *share* the Good News?

*Lord, may we consistently poise our lives for a fresh infilling of the Holy Spirit to see, cry, and care for the needs of Your hurting world.*

## notes

1. Susan Muto, *Pathways of Spiritual Living* (Petersham, Mass.: St. Bede's Publishing, 1984), 31. For further study on the rhythms of contemplation and service, see Muto's book *Renewed at Each Awakening: The Formative Power of Sacred Words* (Denville, N.J.: Dimension Books, 1979).

2. William Barclay, *The Letters of James and Peter, Daily Study Bible Series* (Philadelphia: Westminster Press, 1958), 76.

3. Richard Foster, *Celebration of Discipline* (San Francisco: Harper and Row, 1978), 107.

4. Henri J. M. Nouwen, *Reaching Out* (Garden City, N.Y.: Doubleday, 1975), 58-59.

5. Neill Hamilton, *Maturing in the Christian Life* (Philadelphia: Geneva Press, 1984), 167.

6. Charles R. Swindoll, *Dropping Your Guard: The Value of Open Relationships* (Waco, Tex.: Word Books, 1983), 178.

7. James L. Garlow, *Partners in Ministry* (Kansas City: Beacon Hill Press of Kansas City, 1981), 21.

8. Thomas Gillespie, "The Laity in Biblical Perspective," *The New Laity*, ed. Ralph D. Bucy (Waco, Tex.: Word Books, 1978), 32.

9. Quoted by David Michael Henderson in *John Wesley's In-*

*structional Groups* (Unpublished Ph.D. dissertation, Indiana University, 1980), 124.

10.  John F. Alexander, "The Bible and the Other Side," *The Other Side* 11:5 (September-October 1975), 57.

11.  *The Works of John Wesley,* 3rd ed. (Kansas City: Beacon Hill Press of Kansas City, 1979 reprint of 1872 edition), 5:361-77.

12.  J. Wesley Bready, *England: Before and After Wesley* (London: Hodder and Stoughton, n.d.), 238.

13.  Richard Foster, *Money, Sex and Power* (San Francisco: Harper and Row, 1985), 73.

Janine Tartaglia-Metcalf is the pastor of El Cajon Church of the Nazarene, El Cajon, California. She is a frequent speaker on spiritual formation in workshops, retreats, revivals, and college conventions. This is an adaptation of a chapter first published in *The Upward Call: Spiritual Formation and the Holy Life* (Kansas City: Beacon Hill Press of Kansas City, 1994), 231-44.

# MR. WESLEY, TEACH US THE MISSION AGAIN

## jerry d. porter

**John Wesley fervently wrote** and preached about spiritual disciplines, listing some explicitly, discussing others generally. But no letter or sermon offered more careful instruction in the disciplines than the personal passion that so obviously drove his ministry. Among the primary disciplines he taught by his own life and activity are *evangelism and mission*. These are not optional, secondary disciplines. Sharing our personal testimony and persuading lost friends to embrace life-giving faith in Jesus Christ must be a joyful part of every believer's daily life. Evangelism is not an elective in the curriculum of our Christian development. It is a prerequisite discipline!

Winning the lost is the very nucleus and central focus of our Lord's heart as expressed in the parables and the various great commissionings. Jesus taught us that the creator God of the universe is on a mission to find the lost sheep, the lost coin, and the lost son. We must be compelled by the same mission. Our Lord clearly passed this mission on to His disciples and, implicitly, on to us, when He gave the "great commissions" to His followers.

All authority in heaven and on earth has been given to me. Therefore go and make disciples of all nations, baptizing them in the name of the Father and of the Son and of the Holy Spirit, and teaching them to obey everything I have commanded you. And surely I am with you always, to the very end of the age _(Matt 28:18-20)_.

Go into all the world and preach the good news to all creation. Whoever believes and is baptized will be saved, but whoever does not believe will be condemned _(Mark 16:15-16)_.

This is what is written: The Christ will suffer and rise from the dead on the third day, and repentance and forgiveness of sins will be preached in his name to all nations, beginning at Jerusalem. You are witnesses of these things. I am going to send you what my Father has promised; but stay in the city until you have been clothed with power from on high _(Luke 24:46-49)_.

You will receive power when the Holy Spirit comes on you; and you will be my witnesses in Jerusalem, and in all Judea and Samaria, and to the ends of the earth _(Acts 1:8)_.

Jesus said, "Peace be with you! As the Father has sent me, I am sending you" _(John 20:21)_.

*We often think of John Wesley primarily as a theologian, when in reality he was first and foremost an ardent evangelist.*

Several times and in various settings the Lord emphasized the urgency of fulfilling the divine mission of seeking and finding the lost. This kingdom-of-God "love commission" was a nonnegotiable discipline for John Wesley. During his 50-year ministry he wrote 32 volumes of collected works while preaching the gospel across all of Great Britain, riding more than 250,000 miles on horseback. "From this time, I have, by the grace of God, gone in the same track, travelling between four and five thousand miles a year, and once in two years going through Great Britain and Ireland."[1]

His passion for God and for the lost sparked a holy fire that God used to launch a great renewal movement. We often think of John Wesley primarily as a theologian, when in reality he was first and foremost an ardent evangelist. Were John Wesley with us today, we could ask him for specifics on this calling to evangelism. We could sit at Mr. Wesley's feet and plead, "Teach us the mission again!" In fact his writings show us what he might well say. Listen to the heart of this fervent apostle as we have grouped his teachings into several critically important missional groupings:

## the love of God and neighbor compels our evangelism

John Wesley saw evangelism as the natural response to God's love in our lives. This divine love flows back to God and to neighbor. Evangelism is not a duty, a chore, or an obligation but primarily this natural response to God's love that allows us to love God and others. John Wesley described what it meant to be a genuine Christian: "First, the love of God . . . 'Thou shalt love the Lord thy God with all thy heart, and with all thy soul, and with all thy mind, and with all thy strength' [Mark 12:30, KJV]. Such a love as this occupies the whole heart, takes up all the affections, fills the entire capacity of the soul. . . . The Second thing implied in our being *altogether a Christian* is, the love of our neighbour."[2] "The persons intended by 'our neighbour' are, every child of man, everyone that breathes the vital air, all that have souls to be saved."[3]

Because of God's transforming love, we are compelled to love our neighbors as ourselves and share the gospel with them. John Wesley reminded his brother, Charles, of their highest and primary calling: "Your business as well as mine is to save souls. When we took priests' orders, we undertook to make it our *one business*. I think every day lost which is not (mainly at least) employed in this thing, *Sum totus in illo* (I am completely committed to this)."[4]

God's love in us compels us to love and reach the lost.

## the purified, Christlike heart becomes winsome

Wesley taught the doctrine of Christian perfection where the love of God so fills our lives that all else is dispelled. Teaching and sharing this message of "perfect love" became the calling of the newborn Methodist movement. "This doctrine [full sanctification] is the grand depositum which God has lodged with the people called Methodists; and for the sake of propagating this chiefly He appeared to have raised us up."[5]

The evidence of this holy life makes us winsome and allows the Christian to have grace in the eyes of the lost people around us. Holiness of word and life is characterized by love, humility, and meekness. "Let us first of all take care that whatever we do may be done in 'the spirit of *love;*' in the spirit of tender good-will to our neighbour; as for one who is the son of our common Father, and one for whom Christ died. . . . Meantime the greatest care must be taken that you speak in the spirit of *humility*. . . . If you show, or even feel, the least contempt of those whom you reprove, it will blast your whole work, and occasion you to lose all your labour. . . . Great care must be taken . . . to speak in the spirit of *meekness*. . . . The Apostle assures us that 'the wrath of men worketh not the righteousness of God.'"[6]

The Christlike character of the witness precedes the witnessing.

## evangelism is more relational than verbal

John Wesley knew that effective evangelism did not depend primarily on the specific words that were shared, however theologically correct they may be. The credibility of and quality of relationship with the

> *The evidence of this holy life makes us winsome and allows the Christian to have grace in the eyes of the lost people around us.*

Christian witness are critical variables in reaching the lost with the Good News. This is especially true in these postmodern times when people do not accept absolute truths or values. Everything has become relative. If the Christian witness does not have a good relationship with the lost, the message will not be received. It is precisely the rich relationship between credible believers and their lost family and friends that creates a platform of trust for the effectual presentation of the gospel.

"The holy lives of the Christians will be an argument they will not know how to resist: Seeing the Christians steadily and uniformly practise what is agreeable to the law written in their own hearts, their prejudices will quickly die away, and they will gladly receive 'the truth as it is in Jesus.'"[7]

## we love and relate to our lost neighbor through compassion evangelism

The compassionate response to needy persons is more than an activity Christ's followers choose to do. Compassion becomes a lifestyle that flows from a love-filled heart. A Christian "'does good unto all men;' unto neighbors and strangers, friends and enemies: . . . 'feeding the hungry, clothing the naked, visiting those that are sick or in prison;' [he does much more labor] to do good to their souls, as of the ability which God giveth; to awaken those that sleep in death."[8]

Directly opposite to this [mysticism] is the gospel of Christ. Solitary religion is not to be found here. "Holy solitaries" is a phrase no more consistent with the Gospel than holy adulterers. The

> *Compassion becomes our lifestyle because of God's love at work in our hearts.*

gospel of Christ knows of no religion, but social; no holiness, but social holiness. "Faith working by love" is the length and breadth and depth and height of Christian perfection. "This commandment we have from Christ, that he who loves God, love his brother also;" and that we manifest our love "by doing good unto all men, especially to them that are of the household of faith." And in truth, whosoever loveth his brethren not in work only, but as Christ loved him, cannot but be "zealous of good works." He feels in his soul a burning, restless desire of spending and being spent for them. "My Father," will he say, "worketh hitherto, and I work." And, at all possible opportunities he is, like his Master, "going about doing good."[9]

It is precisely this sincere, pure-hearted compassion in action that makes the Christian message credible and attractive. We do not act compassionately in order to win the lost. Compassion becomes our lifestyle because of God's love at work in our hearts.

## the gospel is extended by each-one-reach-one, lay-driven evangelism

Christian outreach becomes a movement when it has sufficient grassroots traction to move from addition to multiplication. Luke recorded this shift: "The Lord *added* to their number daily those who were being saved" (Acts 2:47, emphasis added). "And the word of God increased; and the number of the disciples *multiplied* in Jerusalem greatly; and a great company of the priests were obedient to the faith" (6:7, KJV, emphasis added). Luke actually goes on to report that the churches multiplied as well: "Then had the churches rest throughout all Judea and Galilee and Samaria, and were edified; and walking in the fear of the Lord, and in the comfort of the Holy Ghost, were *multiplied*" (9:31, KJV, emphasis added).

The exponential growth of the Christian Church takes place when all believers, lay and clergy, embrace the mission of bringing their family and friends to Christ.

"Let us take a view . . . of this Christianity, as *spreading from one to another,* and so gradually making its way into the world. . . . And this our Lord has declared to his first disciples, 'Ye are the salt of the earth,' 'the light of the world' [Matt. 5:13-14, KJV]."[10]

"Meantime, they began to be convinced, that 'by grace we are saved through faith;' that justification by faith was the doctrine of the Church, as well as of the Bible. *As soon as they believed, they spake;* salvation by faith being now their standing topic."[11]

"Ye—Not the apostles, *not ministers only; but all ye who are thus holy, are the salt of the earth*—Are to season others. Ye are the light of the world—If ye are thus holy, you can no more be hid than the sun in the firmament: no more than a city on a mountain. . . . Nay, the very design of God in giving you this light was, that it might shine."[12]

## passion for the lost demands innovative, effective methods

Supposing a few of these lovers of mankind to

*We can be very conservative defending the essence and core message while at the same time being missionally liberal and creative in methods and form.*

see "the whole world lying in wickedness," can we believe they would be unconcerned at the sight, at the misery of those for whom their Lord died? Would not their bowels yearn over them, and their hearts melt away for very trouble? Could they then stand idle all the day long, even were there no command from him whom they loved? Rather, would they not *labour by all possible means,* to pluck some of these brands out of the burning? Undoubtedly they would: they would spare no pains to bring back whomsoever they could of those poor "sheep that have gone astray, to the great Shepherd and Bishop of their souls" (1 Pet. 2:25).[13]

This passion to reach the lost led John Wesley to embrace all possible means and methods that would help accomplish the mission. "I could scarce reconcile myself at first to this strange way of preaching in the fields . . . having been all my life (till very lately) so tenacious of every point relating to decency and order, that I should have thought the saving of souls almost a sin, if it had not been done in a church."[14]

This willingness to be creative and innovative methodologically led John Wesley and his followers to be called "Methodists." We can be very conservative defending the essence and core message while at the same time being missionally liberal and creative in methods and form.

## our mission begins in our homes

From his own childhood Wesley experienced first-hand the love and care of godly parents. He clearly challenged true Christians to prioritize their ministry to their own families before serving the needy world beyond.

> Every real Christian will say, "I and my house will serve the Lord." Who are included in the expression "my house?" The one in your house who claims your first and nearest attention is your *spouse,* seeing you are to love each other as Christ loved the Church. You are to use every possible means that he or she may be free from every spot and walk unblamable in love. Next to your spouse are your *children*—immortal spirits whom God has entrusted to your care for a time that you may train them up in all holiness and fit them for the enjoyment of God for eternity. This is a glorious and important trust, seeing that one soul is of more value than all the world beside. You are, therefore, to watch over every child with the utmost care, that when you are called to give an account of each to the Father of spirits, you may give your accounts with joy and not with grief.[15]

## by God's grace and power, persistent witnessing will produce eternal results

"You that are diligent in this labour of love, see that you be not discouraged, although after you have used your best endeavours, you should see no present fruit. You have need of patience, and then, 'after ye have done the will of God' herein, the harvest will come."[16]

John Wesley believed that patient, persistent witnessing would lead to a precious harvest. This confidence rested not on the skill of the messenger. Wesley taught that God takes the initiative in prevenient grace working in the lives of lost people even before we approach them with the message of hope. His journals are filled with testimonies of people whose hearts were deeply moved with divine conviction. "A young woman followed me into the house, weeping bitterly, and crying out, 'I must have Christ; I will have Christ. Give me Christ, or else I die!' Two or three of us claimed the promise on her behalf. She was soon filled with joy unspeakable, and burst out, 'Oh let me die! Let me go to Him now! How can I bear to stop here any longer?'"[17]

The majestic movement of God often led to emotional manifestations of conviction as well as jubilant outbursts of delight in their newfound faith. "And great indeed was the shaking among them: lamentation and great mourning were heard; God bowing their hearts to that on every side, as with one accord, they lift up their voices and wept aloud."[18]

> While I was enforcing these words, "Be still and know that I am God," He began to make bare His arm, not in a close room, neither in private, but in the open air, and before more than two thousand witnesses. One, and another, and another were struck to the earth, exceedingly trembling at the

presence of His power. Others cried with a loud and bitter cry, "What must we do to be saved?" And in less than an hour seven persons, wholly unknown to me till that time, were rejoicing, and singing, and with all their might giving thanks to the God of their salvation.[19]

John Wesley was not by nature a highly emotional person. He was not always comfortable with these emotional expressions, nevertheless, he attempted to judge people, not by the public emotional manifestations, but by the holy life they lived.

What I have to say touching visions or dreams is this: I know several persons in whom this great change was wrought in a dream, or during a strong representation to the eye of their mind, of Christ either on the cross, or in glory. This is the fact; let any judge of as they please. And that such a change was then wrought appears not from their shedding tears only, or falling into fits, or crying out: these are not the fruits as you seem to suppose, whereby I judge, but from the whole tenor of their life.[20]

We cannot put God in a box. Neither can we easily control people prescribing exactly how they should express their joy in Christ. We lovingly respect these brothers and sisters and recognize that our Lord is at work in their lives. The amazing grace of God is *the primary variable.* We pray, witness, and invite people to embrace faith in Christ. It is, however, from start to finish, the work of God's grace in their hearts that makes the difference.

"But all this time, see that you do not trust in yourself. Put no confidence in your own wisdom, or address, or abilities of any kind. For the success of all you speak or do, trust not in yourself, but in the great Author of every good and perfect gift. Therefore, while you are speaking, continually lift up your heart to him that worketh all in all. And whatsoever is spoken in the spirit of *prayer,* will not fall to the ground."[21] It is all about God's prevenient, convicting, saving, sanctifying, and glorifying grace!

## evangelism implies small-group lifelong discipleship

"This is the great work: not only to bring souls to believe in Christ, but to build them up in our most holy faith. How grievously are they mistaken . . . who imagine that as soon as the children are born they need take no more care of them! We do not find it so. The chief care then begins."[22]

Evangelism is not accomplished and complete when a person comes to faith; but rather integral evangelism includes the whole assignment of "making disciples." During his ministry, John Wesley developed congregational and small-group methods that facilitated the conservation and spiritual growth of new Christians.

In the latter end of the year 1739, eight or ten persons came to me in London, who appeared to be deeply convinced of sin, and earnestly groaning for redemption. They desired (as did two or three more the next day) that I would spend some time with them in prayer, and advise them how to flee from the wrath to come, which they saw continually over their heads; which from thenceforward, they did every week, namely, on Thursday, in the evening. To these, and as many more as desired to join with them (for their number increased daily) I gave those advices, from time to time, which I judged most needful for them; and we always concluded our meeting with prayer suited to their several necessities. This was the rise of the United Society, first of London and then in other places. Such a Society is no other than "a company of men having the form, and seeking the power, of godliness; united, in order to pray together, to receive the word of exhortation, and to watch over one another in love, that they may help each other to work out their salvation."[23]

The societies grew and multiplied, eventually leading to the need for smaller accountability and support groups.

I appointed several earnest and sensible men to meet me, to whom I showed the great difficulty I had long found of knowing the people who desired to be under my care. After much discourse, they all agreed there could be no better way to come to a sure, thorough knowledge of each person than to divide them into classes, like those in Bristol, under the inspection of those in whom I could most confide. This was the origin of our classes at London, for which I can never sufficiently praise God, the unspeakable usefulness of the institution having ever since been more and more manifest.[24]

That it may the more easier be discerned whether they are indeed working out their salvation, each society is divided into smaller companies called _classes_, according to their respective places of abode. There are about twelve persons in each class, one of whom is styled *the Leader*. It is his business, (1) To see each person in his class, once a week at the least, in order to inquire how their souls prosper; to advise, reprove, comfort, or exhort, as occasion may require; to receive what they are willing to give toward the relief of the poor. (2) To meet the Minister and the Stewards of the society once a week; in order to inform the Minister of any that are sick, or of any that are disorderly and will not be reproved; to pay to the stewards what they have received of their several classes in the week preceding.[25]

Wesley further defined the spiritual accountability component of the classes.

These, therefore, wanted some means of closer union; they wanted to pour out their hearts without reserve, particularly with regard to the sin which did still easily beset them and the temptations which were most apt to prevail over them. And they were the more desirous of this when they observed it was the express advice of an inspired writer. "Confess your faults one to another, and pray for one another, that ye may be healed." In compliance with their desire, I divided them into smaller companies; putting the married or single men and married or single women together.[26]

*Today more than ever we need the mutual support and accountability provided by small groups.*

Today more than ever we need the mutual support and accountability provided by small groups. We celebrate in corporate worship but also desperately need the intimate closeness available in "Wesley's classes" in order to mature in the image and character of Christ.

## this global mission includes all people everywhere

From Oxford, where it first appeared, the little leaven spread wider and wider. . . . It afterwards spread to every part of the land, and a little one became a thousand. It then spread into North Britain and Ireland; and, a few years after into New York, Pennsylvania, and many other provinces in America, even as high as Newfoundland and Nova-Scotia. So that, although at first this "grain of mustard seed" was "the least of all the seeds;" yet, in a few years, it grew into a "large tree, and put forth great branches."[27]

"Go ye into all the world, and preach the Gospel to every creature—Our Lord speaks without any limitation or restriction."[28]

This gospel is for all people everywhere. There are no preferred races, nationalities, languages, or social classes at the foot of the Cross. The mission is not just to reach our immediate "Jerusalem" culture but to carry the Good News to all persons everywhere.

Wesley speaks to our present-day evangelism and mission challenges as clearly as if he were still preaching among us. Some view his teaching as primarily a call to holy living, but he obviously taught that _the call to be holy is also a call to mission._ We often accentuate personal heart purity without equal emphasis on the power of the Holy Spirit to witness to people culturally near and far. Wesley's repetitive teaching of our two-dimensional love of God and neighbor calls us both to holy living and to evangelism. John Wesley rediscovered and contextualized the God-blessed methods of the New Testament that allowed for a mighty awakening in his day. Today, we enthusiastically embrace the Wesleyan discipline of evangelism as we passionately, personally, persistently, winsomely, compassionately, and creatively touch the lives of those around us with God's transforming Good News.

## notes

1. John Wesley, *The Works of John Wesley,* ed. Thomas Jackson, 3d ed. (1872; reprint, Peabody, Mass.: Hendrickson Publishers, 1984), 13:380.

2. John Wesley, Sermon 2, "The Almost Christian."

3. John Wesley, Sermon 65, "The Duty of Reproving Our Neighbour."

4. John Wesley, *Letters* (April 20, 1772).

5. Ibid. (September 15, 1790).

6. Wesley, Sermon 65, "The Duty of Reproving Our Neighbour."

7. John Wesley, Sermon 63, "The General Spread of the Gospel."

8. Wesley, *Works,* 8:346.

9. Ibid., 14:321-22.

10. John Wesley, Sermon 4, "Scriptural Christianity," emphasis added.

11. Wesley, *Works,* 8:349, emphasis added.

12. John Wesley, *Explanatory Notes on the New Testament,* Matthew 5:13-15, emphasis added.

13. Wesley, Sermon 4, "Scriptural Christianity," emphasis added.

14. John Wesley's *Journal* (March 29, 1739).

15. John Wesley, Sermon 94, "On Family Religion."

16. Wesley, Sermon 65, "The Duty of Reproving Our Neighbour."

17. John Wesley's *Journal* (September 3, 1775).

18. Ibid. (June 11, 1742).

19. Ibid. (May 20, 1739).

20. Ibid.

21. Wesley, Sermon 65, "The Duty of Reproving Our Neighbour."

22. Wesley, *Letters* (November 4, 1772).

23. Wesley, *Works,* 8:269.

24. John Wesley's *Journal* (April 25, 1742).

25. Wesley, *Works,* 8:269-70.

26. Ibid., 258.

27. Wesley, Sermon 63, "The General Spread of the Gospel."

28. Wesley, *Explanatory Notes on the New Testament,* Mark 16:15.

Jerry D. Porter is a general superintendent in the Church of the Nazarene. This chapter is an expansion of an article first published in *Holiness Today,* January 2004.

# RELATIONSHIPS: NOT AN OPTION

## dana preusch

**My friend Misty has struggled** with an alcohol addiction for most of her life. She has a passion for God and a passion for ministry that is incredibly inspiring. Yet her childhood memories of sexual and verbal abuse have often driven her to alcohol as an escape.

Thankfully, faithful friends have locked arms with Misty over the years and have supported her on her journey to healing and wholeness. These *spiritual* friends have helped her make great strides. They presented a compelling picture of Christianity and the church that was attractive to her, and they invited her to join their small group. It was in this small group that Misty found she could celebrate the good times and successes of her journey. The small group also became a place where she could go when she faltered and needed support. Eventually Misty grew enough in her faith so that she wanted to attend church, and to-

day she is a committed servant, shepherd-
ing a small group of fifth and sixth graders,
helping them grow in the faith and into
adulthood.

Misty could have read the Bible through
every year, fasted weekly, and prayed daily
throughout the last seven years she has
been with our church. Yet without her spiritual friendships, she never would have
achieved the spiritual maturity and success
over her circumstances that she did.

It is ironic that some Christians, who
would never dispute the need for Bible
study, prayer, and worship in the life of a
believer, resist the idea that Christians need
*each other* to grow. Unfortunately, the indi-
vidualism that pervades our larger culture
has seeped into our churches, convincing
many of us that we can indeed go it alone.
But Misty reminds us that spiritual friendships are critical to each one of us on the
journey of faith. The clear mandate of
Scripture and the example of the Early
Church should also give us pause when we
are tempted to limit the engines of spiritual
growth to those disciplines that are practiced individually.

*It is ironic that some Christians, who would never dispute the need for Bible study, prayer, and worship in the life of a believer, resist the idea that Christians need each other to grow.*

John reminds us in his Gospel that relationships
are not optional: "Dear friends, let us continue to love
one another, for love comes from God. . . . This is real
love. It is not that we loved God, but that he loved us
and sent his Son as a sacrifice to take away our sins.

[So] dear friends, since God loves us that much, we surely ought to love each other. No one has ever seen God. But if we love each other, God lives in us, and his love has been brought to full expression through us" (1 John 4:7, 10-12, NLT).

God's love was certainly brought to "full expression" through the believers in the first-century Church. Acts 2 is an astounding picture of community and spiritual growth. The first Christians met for worship *daily,* not weekly. They spent significant time together. They loved each other in radical ways. They shared with each other not only their meals and possessions but also their very lives. And the caliber of the community and of each believer in it was so winsome and compelling that outsiders looking in just couldn't resist! "And each day the Lord added to their group those who were being saved" (v. 47, NLT).

Verse 47 and the experience of my friend Misty remind us of the critical importance that relationships play in a person's conversion. In my experience as a pastor, *relationships* are indeed key to convincing others of the love of Christ and, also, of our love for them. For my friend Misty, her small group nurtured a budding faith in her that eventually blossomed into a full-blown commitment to Christ and His Church. She would not have come to Christ on her own. Being a part of the community and building spiritual friendships was the critical factor in her coming to faith in Christ. And in the postmodern world where we live, reaching people at this heartfelt, emotional level is a nonnegotiable. Reaching people through relationships is just as important as intellectually convincing them of the truth of the gospel. In sum, the Church will be most effective in fulfilling its first-order mission—reaching lost persons—through the avenue of *relationships.*

But relationships also play a key role in the spiritual growth of those who make a commitment to the faith. Relationships are critical for the development and nurture of all Christians who truly want to love God with all their heart, mind, soul, and strength—and their neighbor as themselves. Relationships—spiritual friendships, more specifically—are not optional but necessary for growing believers into Acts 2 kind of people—winsome persons who bear the fruit of the Spirit (love, joy, peace, patience, kindness) and display an alternate way of living that is attractive and compelling to the outside world.

John Wesley understood the power of small-group ministry. For him, small groups, or class meetings, proved to be not only "mediators" of conversions but also places where significant spiritual growth happened. Wesley became a participant in successful mass evangelism efforts to the unchurched at the invitation of the popular preacher George Whitefield. However, the spiritual revolution they birthed in England in the 1700s became more strongly associated with Wesley than Whitefield for one crucial reason: Wesley organized small groups for new believers, while Whitefield left it up to the individual to take the initiative for spiritual growth. As a result, Wesley's converts grew and thrived in their Christian faith, while many of Whitefield's faltered. Knowing that relationships were essential for spiritual growth, Wesley organized small groups according to levels of Christian maturity and urged each group to foster an intimate community where the highs and lows of each believer's spiritual journey could be shared in confidence. The group was to be a place of accountability and challenge concerning sin and temptation, as well as a place of encouragement, love, and support.

Wesley's small-group strategy played a key role in not only the spiritual transformation of thousands upon thousands of working-class people but also the *moral* reform of a whole nation—at precisely the time when other nations were in a state of social upheaval and chaos. While other European nations in the 18th century were being torn apart by revolutionary wars, England flourished. Many historians credit this to the work of John Wesley. Spiritual and social transformation happened because Wesley grasped the value of *spiritual* friendships and put an effective system in place to foster this kind of spiritual discipline and nurture. D. Michael Henderson writes, "John Wesley was able to cut through the trappings of Anglicanism and recapture the spirit of koinonia, the supportive fellowship of primitive Christianity. Those who are committed to making disciples in the world of the twenty-first century will do well to learn from him."[1] Wesley emphasized what the earliest Christians already knew—true and lasting life change happens almost always in the context of *spiritual* relation-

> *Relationships were not optional for the Early Church, nor for John Wesley, and they should not be optional for us now.*

ships. Relationships were not optional for the Early Church, nor for John Wesley, and they should not be optional for us now.

I believe that *now* is the exact right time in our culture and in our churches for new and growing believers to embrace this concept that spiritual growth will not happen if we rely solely on those disciplines that are practiced individually. For a postmodern generation that highly values relationships and community, the time certainly seems to be right. Baby busters and the millennials, and others who follow, must contend with an increasingly fragmented and broken world. With the divorce rate reaching 50 percent in our country, blended families and households led by single parents are more and more the norm. Thus the postmodern generations long to recapture and restore relationships that they have lost along the way. They desire security and longevity in their relationships, as well as a place to call home. This was certainly my friend Misty's experience. Although her parents never divorced, the abuse she experienced in her home left her uneasy about trusting others. She simply didn't feel safe in relationships—especially not with God. And, so, it took a long-term commitment on the part of her spiritual friends to help her come back to a place where she could eventually trust God and other people. Her small group was a place where she could finally and fully belong. Her small group became a place where she could tell her story. It became a place she could call home.

Thankfully, over the course of the last few decades, many new and existing churches have worked diligently to create spaces where spiritual friendships can be formed through the avenue of small groups. My own church began 13 years ago as a plant, and small groups have always been an important part of the DNA. In my church, small groups have often been formed by the affinity of the people in them. Shared life circumstances and family or marital status have always been natural ways to group people. At my church, we have offered specific invitations to persons to attend "sampler" small-group events at regular and strategic intervals, such as in the fall or at the first of the year, when persons are ready to make new commitments. These events are designed to give new persons a "taste" of what they might experience at a small-group meeting and are a nonthreatening way for people to begin to get to know each other. We try to start new groups on a regular basis but also provide places for interested persons to land in already existing groups throughout any given church year. Placements of new persons in existing groups are made on a case-by-case basis in consultation with a group leader and the members of the group.

The curriculum and meeting structure of each group will vary. Lay pastors are given lots of flexibility in "designing" their groups. Some groups will choose to stress content and will resemble more of a traditional Sunday School class. Other groups will choose to focus more on relationship building and accountability in specific areas of life—for example, marriage, parenting, spiritual life, and so on. Each lay pastor is given help in customizing a curriculum strategy that will help his or her group accomplish its goals. A weekly curriculum based on the sermon texts is also made available to the small groups.

Each lay pastor is also accountable to a lay pastor "coach" for what curriculum is being used and what his or her group goals are, as well as other group dynamics (relationship building, outreach, service, worship, etc.). Lay pastor coaches oversee five to six small groups and contact their lay pastors on a regular basis to review progress in these areas. Coaches also meet on a regular basis to share information about each of their groups and also to pray and plan larger training sessions. Training sessions are held on a quarterly basis and consist of a specific face-to-face time for coaches to meet with the leaders of the groups they oversee (called "huddles"). The quarterly sessions are also times for training in specific areas for the lay pastor—for example, "how to lead more effective group discussions," "how to counsel members of your group who are hurting," "dealing with problem people," and so on.

Although we employ more "traditional" types of small groups at my church, there are also other new and compelling models out there that may be even more effective at forging deep, spiritual friendships. For example, in his book *The Connecting Church,* Pastor Randy Frazee of Pantego Bible Church in Arlington, Texas, has advocated a fresh and creative approach to small-group ministry that stresses the importance of neighborhood groups and a small-group structure that is integrated into the larger life of the church. Worship, education, and small-group ministry are interconnected and reinforce one another. Frazee's model is especially compelling because reducing geographical dis-

tance between group members increases their chances
of meeting with each other more regularly. Frequency
of interaction builds the trust and confidence needed
among group members for them to begin sharing life
at a deeper level.

However, having said all of this about the importance of small groups as a necessary spiritual discipline in the life of the believer, and after having been
intimately involved with small-group ministry for over
a decade, I still would offer some cautions regarding
the efficacy of small groups. Although I don't sub-
scribe to his arguments as a whole, I believe that Joseph R. Myers offers some compelling cautions to
those who would embrace small groups as the only
place or structure where important spiritual relationships can be formed. In his book *The Search to Belong:
Rethinking Intimacy, Community and Small Groups,*
Myers debunks the notion that small groups are the
*"end-all" solution,* saying, "Small groups do not accomplish the promise of fulfilling all facets of a person's
search for community. Small groups deliver only on
one or two specific kinds of connection. A person's
search for community is more complex than this. The
truth is that people can experience belonging in
groups ranging in size from two to 2,000 or more. People have competencies to pursue many different paths
in their search for community."[2]

Myers goes on to outline four different "spaces"
where various levels of relationship connections can
be made. These include public, social, personal, and
intimate settings that he defines literally by the
amount of actual space taken up in each interaction.

Public space, for example, is defined as being separated from a person by 12 or more feet, while intimate distance, on the other end of the spectrum, is 0 to 18 inches. Myers argues that the church should make room for the viable "spaces" where successful and authentic community can be established other than "personal" and "intimate" space, which is where most small groups want to concentrate. He contends that immediate and lasting connections can also be made in public and social settings.

For instance, significant friendships can occur in a Sunday School class. Although these types of group settings tend to be more _content_ rather than relationship focused, that "space" (less personal and more public) can easily become a place of belonging for someone less comfortable with more intimate settings. Thus a Sunday School class can provide a place of belonging for someone who might never be willing to join a small group. The classroom setting may prove to be a less threatening "space." It could easily, however, serve as a stepping-stone, too, for a person who might eventually join a small group and seek to build even deeper intimacy with others. But Myers's contention, in sum, is that belonging is "multidimensional." Again, the small group is not the "end-all" solution. Other kinds of relationships that occur in different kinds of "spaces" can be just as significant and important for our overall emotional and spiritual well-being.

And relationships that happen to be _structured_ a bit differently than the typical small-group meeting can also play a key role in someone's spiritual development. Mentoring relationships are potentially good examples of this. The concept of mentoring has received a lot of positive attention in recent years, and many churches have gotten serious about creating spaces where these kinds of relationships can flourish. My own church has recently implemented a financial mentoring program as well as a MOPS (mothers of preschoolers) program, both of which are specifically structured to foster relationships of support, encouragement, and guidance among a variety of generations and life experiences. We are also considering the formation of a marriage-mentoring program.

Much more could be said about each of the relationship types and "spaces" mentioned above, but when all is said and done, for the Christian—relationships are not optional. My friend Misty thrives as a Christian believer now primarily because of her spiritual friendships. Yes, there are times she still falters—but friends are always there to pick her up. Her friends have, in turn, given her the strength to reach out to others who are hurting and don't know Christ. Her spiritual friendships have given her the courage she needs to mentor and teach fifth and sixth graders, even in those times when she feels like a failure. Yes, Misty could have read the Bible through every year, fasted weekly, and prayed daily, but without her spiritual friendships, she never would have achieved the spiritual maturity and success over her circumstances that she has gained. God's love has indeed been brought to "full expression" in Misty.

"Dear friends, let us continue to love one another, for love comes from God. . . . This is real love. It is not that we loved God, but that he loved us and sent his Son as a sacrifice to take away our sins. [So] dear friends, since God loves us that much, we surely ought to love each other. No one has ever seen God. But if we love each other, God lives in us, and his love has been brought to full expression through us" (1 John 4:7, 10-12, NLT).

## notes

1. D. Michael Henderson, *John Wesley's Class Meetings: A Model for Making Disciples* (Nappanee, Ind.: Evangel Publishing House, 1997), 15.

2. Joseph R. Myers, *The Search to Belong: Rethinking Intimacy, Community and Small Groups* (Grand Rapids: Zondervan Publishing Company), 2003.

Dana Preusch, while on staff at Christ Community Church of the Nazarene in Olathe, Kansas, worked with the church's small-group ministry for almost a decade. This chapter is an expansion of an article first published in *Holiness Today*, January 2004.

# THE DISCIPLINED COMMUNITY

## edwin de jong

### team players

Basketball, hockey, volleyball, a relay race, and baseball—what do these sports have in common? At first, this list may just seem to be a random collection of popular sports. But when you take the time to think about it, the answer to this question is not hard—all these sports are played in a team. A team sport, by definition, is played by more than one person. In Europe, for example, by far the most popular team sport is soccer. Nothing gets the blood pumped up and a good conversation going like an exciting game on the soccer field. Millions of people watch soccer games on television, and the newspapers on Monday are filled with lengthy reports of the matches played over the weekend. Soccer certainly is a big thing in Europe.

Like all other athletes, soccer players need a fair amount of skill and natural talent, but skill and talent alone are not enough to make a player a real star. Success for any sports star comes at the price of regular and disciplined practice. When discipline fails, performance suffers. But even a soccer star with a world of talent and the discipline to practice every day cannot do the job alone. Soccer, like every other team sport, transcends discipline and personal skill because in a team sport what really counts is the performance of the team. I've always thought it interesting that even teams with less talented players can still beat better-ranked opponents when they try hard not to be just a group of talented individuals but rather a unified team that places team spirit over everything else.

Much of this carries over into our spiritual lives. Just as sports stars need disciplined practice to improve their performance, we as Christians need a disciplined spirituality to improve our obedience to God. But the comparison doesn't stop here. Every one of us may be convinced of the importance of the *personal* spiritual disciplines but still not be a *team player*. In the kingdom of God, however, the team, or what we normally call the church, is of utmost importance. Just as team sports are designed to be played in a team, the Christian life is designed to be lived in a community of faith. If we truly long to experience the joy of living in God's presence, we must

*Just as team sports are designed to be played in a team, the Christian life is designed to be lived in a community of faith.*

recognize and embrace the reality that the Christian life is lived out in community. Or to put it a little differently: Christians are team players.

I like to include going to church and being an active and faithful member of your congregation among the spiritual disciplines. It is a spiritual discipline practiced in community. For many of us the word "discipline" has an ambivalent meaning. On the one hand, it seems to convey a sense of obligation, often related to things that we do not automatically put on the top of our to-do lists. We need discipline to do things we actually do not want to do. On the other hand, we know, even though we are not always ready to admit it, that discipline is good for us. Without discipline, many of us do not get out of bed voluntarily and we only bring out the garbage after the neighbors have complained about the smell. Discipline helps us to live the life we ought and want to live.

Most of the times, this is not any different with spiritual disciplines. We know these disciplines will help us to live healthy spiritual lives, but we may still not be overtly thrilled to implement them into our daily routine. This also applies to the spiritual discipline of community. Let's be honest: some of us need a fair amount of discipline to be faithful members of our local church. Some 2,000 years ago, the author of Hebrews warned us already not to give up meeting together, as some were obviously in the habit of doing (Heb. 10:25). And that is not any different now. As a matter of fact, many people today have decided not to go to church anymore. Instead, they believe it is possible to live out their faith within the walls of their private homes by watching Robert Schuler and his *Hour of Power* on Sunday morning television. But anyone who believes he or she doesn't need the church is either arrogant or ignorant. No person, book, or television program can serve as an excuse for Christians to neglect the God-given commandment to be an active part of a local faith community. To be a Christian means to be part of the church. Christians are team players.

## community

One of the themes that has appealed to fiction writers throughout history is that of a lonely man trying to survive on a deserted island. Probably the best-known book exploring this idea is Daniel Defoe's *Robinson Crusoe*. In short, the story goes like this: A man is sailing on a ship somewhere in the tropics and is caught in a violent storm. The storm is so brutal that the ship goes down, and as the only survivor the man is washed on the shores of a deserted island. Initially we feel sorry for his pitiful fate, but as it turns out, the island isn't so bad after all. There are many streams with fresh water; coconuts and other ripe fruits are falling from the trees; and the sea is full of fat fish that can be grilled above a romantic campfire. On first impression, the stranded survivor seems to live in a perfect world. There is plenty to eat and drink, the sun is always shining, and the island resembles the pictures of an advertisement brochure. But think about it—isn't it interesting that most people who are stranded on a deserted island want to leave this seemingly perfect place and return to the inhabited world?

The reality is that each of us is created with a desire for social interaction. We need other people in our life. Around the year 300 B.C., Aristotle already remarked that humankind, by nature, is a "social animal," and psychologists tell us that we are all part of a social network built of countless relationships. Because our social relations seem so natural to us, it is sometimes difficult to appreciate just how much we depend on other people, but whenever you doubt the importance of relationships in your own life, try spending a few days completely alone!

The very human need for fellowship and community has not just been recognized by psychologists and philosophers but is also part of the biblical message. In the very beginning of Scripture, the Bible tells us that God looked at Adam and realized it was not good for him to be alone (Gen. 2:18). People have longed for companionship from the time of their creation because God created us with the desire to be with other people. In fact, the Scriptures teach us that there is no other way to live the Christian life but to do so in community. The apostle Paul, in his first letter to the congregation in Corinth, compared the church with a physical body, and he explained how each part of the body contributes to the whole and at the same time depends on the other parts. Do you remember a particular time when you broke an arm or a leg, or did something else that forced you to wear a cast for several weeks? It is only when you are unable to use a particular part of your body that you realize how much it contributes to the whole. Because Paul wanted to make absolutely sure that his readers would understand what he meant, he added: "Now *you* are the body of Christ, and each one of *you* is a part of it" (1 Cor. 12:27, emphasis added). This was as true for the people in Corinth as it is for us—you and I, we, are members in God's church! This means that for us as Christians, going to church is not optional. Going to church is a spiritual discipline.

True, being a member of God's family can be a real challenge at times. None of us probably needs to think very long before we're able to recall some moments or actions within the church community that hurt or disappointed us. In one way or another, we have all experienced occasions when the church was not always the sanctified community we would like it to be. I am sure one of the reasons David was so convinced that it is good and pleasant when brothers and sisters live together in unity (Ps. 133:1) was because it did not happen very often. But community means not only living together when everything seems to be perfect but also sticking with each other when there are tensions, disagreements, and problems.

The church at its heart is a community of believers. This is also reflected in the functions of the church. When you read through the whole New Testament, it becomes very obvious that many functions of the church are community functions. The words "one another," for example, appear

*Community means not only living together when everything seems to be perfect but also sticking with each other when there are tensions, disagreements, and problems.*

dozens of times in the New Testament. We are called to love one another, pray for one another, forgive one another, accept one another, serve one another, share with one another, and encourage one another. One biblical term expressing the fellowship or community we experience in the church is the Greek word *koinonia,* which can also be translated as "participation" or "sharing in something." In the church we all share and participate in fellowship with other believers. To be a part of the church means to live in community.

## worship

Clearly the human dimension of community is very important, yet in the church, community means more than just being together with other people. Community in the church also means dwelling in the presence of God. Whether or not we think about God, whether we sit in the service, eat together, or meet with the youth group, God is always part of our community. Jesus promised us that whenever two or three come together in His name, He would be there with them (Matt. 18:20). Often this verse has been limited to encouraging small groups, such as the one that shows up for the Sunday night prayer meeting, but that was not its original intention. What Jesus is saying here is that He will be with us whenever we meet in His name.

Several years ago, my wife and I spent a week in Venice, Italy, a very old and fascinating city. When you walk through its narrow alleys or cross the beautiful open squares, it feels as if nothing for the last 500 years has changed. Because Venice is built on many small islands, the city is surrounded by water and you are always close to one of the Venetian-style bridges crossing the city's many canals. Venice, however, is known not just for its many canals but also for its many churches. One day we visited Saint Mark's cathedral, one of the city's largest and most famous churches. We were there relatively early and wanted to visit the morning service. The service was not held in the large, century-old sanctuary, as we had assumed, but in a small room somewhere in the back of the building. When the service was over, we walked back to the main sanctuary and noticed that the whole church was full of people. From all over the world people came to this church to admire its architecture and the beautiful paintings decorating its interior. The church's main purpose, however, to be a house of worship, had become irrelevant to most of its visitors.

*There is no better way to express our love for God than through worship.*

I believe that corporate worship is an important part of the spiritual discipline of community and an integral part of the local church. There is no better way to express our love for God than through worship. Worship can take many forms, but the primary setting for worship is the local church where God's people gather in obedient service to Him. It is as we are gathered before God in worship—singing, hearing the public reading of the Bible, giving our tithes and offerings, praying, listening to the preached Word, baptizing, and sharing the Lord's Supper—that we know most clearly what it means to be the people of God. The Scriptures are filled with statements that record God's invitation to worship and God's expectations of a worshiping congregation. To put it briefly, worship is a necessity for the people of God.

Even though this chapter is not about worship, but about the spiritual discipline of community, I would like to make two comments about worship in our churches. First of all, worship is not about us, but about a faith community focused on God. In our present times there is a very strong and regrettable emphasis on the individual, almost to the extent that the social and communal dimensions in our lives are forgotten. This unfortunately also applies to our experiences in worship. It is true that worship is a channel for God's grace to work in our lives, and it is also true that we can worship God individually. But we must realize that something very powerful and moving occurs when we cross our personal boundaries and worship in community. Can you even begin to imagine the blessings that result from offering God your gift of worship together and simultaneously with brothers and sisters in Christ?

Second, many churches are struggling with the question of what style of worship to choose for their Sunday morning worship service. The options basically range from traditional hymns accompanied by the organ, on the one hand, to contemporary choruses and modern music, on the other. Even though most churches probably fit somewhere in between these two ends, it is still possible that many in the church are distracted by, or even upset with, the style of worship. Let me remind you, however, that there is no

right way of worshiping God. Also, we do not worship
for personal gain, but we worship God purely for the
sake of worshiping God. In the Gospel of John, Jesus
gave only two requirements for worship that is pleasing to His Father: "God is spirit, and his worshipers
must worship in spirit and in truth" (John 4:24). Too
often different groups of worshipers have fought an
"unholy war" over their personal worship preferences.
In the end, however, this has only distracted worshipers from their duty and divided the community. We
must recognize that to be a member of the church
means to be part of a worshiping community. In the
church we worship God.

## the Lord's supper

Perhaps the best expression of the fellowship we
experience through the spiritual discipline of community is the joyful celebration of the Lord's Supper.
Imagine this—when we eat from the bread and drink
from the cup we are one with all believers because we
are united in Jesus Christ. Paul wrote to the Corinthians, "No matter how many of us there are, we all eat
from the same loaf, showing that we are all parts of
the one body of Christ" (1 Cor. 10:17, TLB). The Lord's
Supper is a community meal.

When I was a little boy and went to church with
my parents, there were several important factors that
determined the success of my Sunday mornings in
church. First of all, there was the question of whether
or not my friends would be there to play with. Second,
in my opinion a good service always had cookies to go
with the coffee after the morning worship. And third, a

successful Sunday morning required a short service. Because of this third success factor, I always was a little unhappy when I noticed we were planning to celebrate Communion. The sanctuary of the church I attended was quite large with the entrance all the way in the back. Whenever I would enter the church and see the tables with the white tablecloths standing in the front, I knew a short service would be out of the question.

Traditionally, in many cultures in the Middle East, the time people spend around the table to share a meal together is very important. Often, the whole family will gather, and much more than in western cultures, the meal is a social event and as such an important part of daily life. When all are seated around the table and the food is shared, there is time to share the local rumors, have fellowship with one another, and talk about the most important news.

When we realize that the sharing of a meal still plays an important role in the cultures of the Middle East, we may understand why people in biblical times took eating very seriously. In different places we read that when guests would come by, the fattened calf would be killed and a banquet prepared. Even when the guests dropped by unexpectedly, they would not be sent away but were received with open arms and friendly faces. Meals were a means to express mutual respect and appreciation. Just imagine that you're having friends over for dinner. You or your spouse have carefully selected the menu, gotten all the groceries, and decorated the table. Now the food is almost ready and your friends are about to arrive. Now think about this question: why did you invite your friends to come over in the first place? What are your expectations for this evening? Probably you were not just motivated by the food that would be served, because on occasions like these it seems that the sharing of the meal is even more important than the meal itself. I would therefore guess that you were expecting a great evening with nice company and good fellowship, "because nothing is better for a man under the sun than to eat and drink and be glad" (Eccles. 8:15). From this small example we may conclude that the primary function of a meal is not always to fill the stomach. Sometimes what we expect of a meal is to experience friendship, hospitality, and fellowship with one another.

When we think of the Lord's Supper, we do not usually think of an actual meal that we share around the table with some of our closest friends. As a matter of fact, the way we celebrate Communion in our churches nowadays, with very little to eat and drink, only helps to sever the connection between the Lord's Supper and a real evening dinner. But very much like a dinner we share with good friends, the Lord's Supper started as an evening meal among a very intimately connected group of people. And just as the food we serve during an evening with friends is only of secondary importance, so the food at the Lord's Supper wasn't really the main thing.

When the 12 disciples together with Jesus found themselves in the Upper Room, they had prepared themselves to celebrate the Passover meal. And while they were eating, Jesus took the bread, blessed it, broke it, and gave it to His disciples. And after they

*The Lord's Supper is a communal celebration and a visible sign of God's gracious presence in the midst of His community.*

had finished eating, Jesus also took the cup and passed it around, so that all could drink from it. I believe that the disciples would probably never forget the meal they shared on this evening, even though it wasn't really the meal itself that was most important. It was because of what Jesus said and did that the meal took on new meaning.

The Lord's Supper is a communal celebration and a visible sign of God's gracious presence in the midst of His community. John Wesley once referred to the Lord's Supper as the "grand channel" whereby the worshiping community is blessed with the presence of the Holy Spirit. While partaking of the elements, believers may find in the Lord's Supper not only a fresh and new encounter with God's empowering grace but also a new awareness of what it means to be part of God's community. To be part of the church means to share in the Lord's Supper.

## conclusion

Consider this—most of us who worship together on Sunday morning would probably have never met if God hadn't brought us all together in His church. It is fascinating to see how people who differ from one another in many ways find their place within the same church. Probably the church is the only place where we find such a wide variety of people who have nothing else in common but their shared convictions about God and His community. Just once, look around you while worshiping with your brothers and sisters, and you will see an encouraging variety of people. There may be people of many different races and nationalities. There may be people who have spent their whole life in the same church, as well as people who only joined the community very recently, searching for a place to worship. When you look a little closer, you may even notice older and younger generations standing side by side and observe how newly converted Christians are supported and encouraged by more mature Christians. God's variety in His family is something wonderful and continues to amaze us.

It is a real privilege to be an active and faithful member of the community of God. When we stress the importance of the spiritual disciplines, let us not forget the spiritual discipline of community. Through fellowship and community, joyous worship, and reverent acceptance of the bread and the cup, God desires to flood the Church with His empowering grace and awesome blessing! You and I can be a part of this. Let's be team players in the community of God.

Edwin de Jong is pastor of the Church of the Nazarene in Gottmadingen, Germany, and part-time lecturer at European Nazarene College. This chapter is an expansion of an article first published in *Holiness Today*, January 2004.

# ONCE DELIVERED AND CONTINUALLY PRACTICED

## henry w. spaulding II

**The Christian faith seeks to produce** a peculiar people by telling a particular story. These people in turn are answerable to God to faithfully hand down this redemptive story to others. Jude 3 urges us to "contend for the faith that was once for all entrusted to the saints" (NRSV). As Christians we become stewards of this Christian faith, or tradition, and pass it on from one generation to the next through the practice of formative preaching and teaching inspired by the Holy Spirit. Yet not only inspiration but also perspiration is needed to reach another generation. As Moses stood at the end of his life and the threshold of the conquest of Canaan, he urged the new generation to "keep the commandments of the LORD your God, and his decrees, and his statutes that he has commanded you" (Deut. 6:17, NRSV). Moses suggested that when the children of the new generation needed to understand the meaning of these commandments, decrees, and statutes, the story of the Exodus would explain them. Likewise, it is the stories of the faith that engender Christian life in every generation. It is their continual retelling through the practice of formative preaching and teaching that prepares God's people to engage life faithfully.

We should thus understand formative preaching and teaching to be once delivered and continually practiced. It is not enough for the message to have once upon a time been spoken; it must be rehearsed and practiced in every new generation. As an attempt to extend a clearer understanding of this, we will do four things: First, we will look at the precise meaning of formative preaching. Second, we will explore what it means to talk about preaching and teaching as a practice of the Christian faith. Third, we will address the importance of listening. Finally, we will look at the role of friendship that is fostered by sound preaching and teaching. Through this study it's important to keep in mind that only an embodied faith will have the capacity to endure amid the complexity of our lives.

## the meaning of formative preaching and teaching

One of the oldest definitions of theology is "faith seeking understanding." In other words, a faith born through the preaching of the Word reaches out to be understood. Paul proclaims to the Corinthians, "When I came to you, brothers and sisters, I did not come proclaiming the mystery of God to you in lofty words or wisdom" (1 Cor. 2:1, NRSV). He adds to this "My speech and my proclamation were not with plausible words of wisdom, but with a demonstration of the Spirit and of power" (v. 4, NRSV). A careless reading of these verses might lead us to conclude that the sole purpose of preaching is to open the door to faith but rarely to "seek understanding." We might even read it as an attempt to dismiss serious study and thinking regarding the faith. This is a conclusion that Paul clearly refutes: "Yet among the mature we do speak wisdom, though it is not a wisdom of this age or of the rulers of this age, who are doomed to perish" (v. 6, NRSV). Formative preaching and teaching defines a wisdom that reaches to the mature and prepares a person to live the kind of life that will endure in the face of all challenges. In other words, when preaching and teaching is understood in the richest sense, the whole gamut of Christian grace comes into view. We can see the gray hair and wrinkled faces of those who have been faithful disciples of Jesus for many years. Formative preaching and teaching thus shares the gospel in such a way that God's people will know and embody the virtues of the Christian faith.

Formative preaching and teaching, in

> *Formative preaching and teaching shares the gospel in such a way that God's people will know and embody the virtues of the Christian faith.*

the power of the Spirit, forms Christian character. Paul exhorts his spiritual son Timothy, "Have nothing to do with profane myths and old wives' tales. Train yourself in godliness, for, while physical training is of some value, godliness is valuable in every way, holding promise for both the present life and the life to come" (1 Tim. 4:7-8, NRSV). Paul is emphasizing the importance of being formed by a story, a message, that can produce the kind of life that is lasting. Such a life will be a fragrant offering in the presence of God. Formative preaching and teaching sustains Christian character. It subverts "profane myths and old wives' tales." In fact, only the Christian story will finally stand in the face of secular challenges.

The New Testament is filled with formative preaching and teaching. Paul addressed issues such as law and grace, spiritual gifts, and the Second Coming. The writer of Hebrews addressed the superiority of the Christian faith in light of angels and all other priesthoods (Melchizedek's and Aaron's). James addressed the separation of faith and works. The writer of 1 John urges Christians to test spirits. These are only a few of the issues addressed in the New Testament, yet they show that the New Testament is concerned with the kind of preaching and teaching that forms Christian character. The same case could be made for the preaching of the prophets who call God's people to covenantal faithfulness.

Formative preaching and teaching is wrapped up with a specific content: the law, the prophets, the wisdom, the gospel, and the story of the Church. Put simply, formative preaching and teaching concerns the telling of the story of Israel, the story of Jesus, and the story of the Church. It is the Church's deep conviction that telling these stories gives the faithful the resources needed to form Christian character.

Paul urges the Colossians, "As you therefore have received Christ Jesus the Lord, continue to live your lives in him, rooted and built up in him and established in the faith, just as you were taught, abounding in thanksgiving" (2:6-7, NRSV). Formative preaching and teaching is framed by the gospel and as such reaches deep into the heart. Faith joins head and heart. The content and practice of the Christian faith is connected to the delicate tissues of life. First Peter 1:13-16 makes this point clear:

> Therefore prepare your minds for action; discipline yourselves; set all your hope on the grace that Jesus Christ will bring you when he is revealed. Like obedient children, do not be conformed to the desires that you formerly had in ignorance. Instead, as he who called you is holy, be holy yourselves in all your conduct; for it is written. "You shall be holy, for I am holy" (NRSV).

Here we find the essential elements of the practice of formative preaching and teaching. First, action arises from a mind prepared by the specific content of the gospel. Second, the mind and heart are disciplined by the continual telling and retelling of the stories of the faith. This brings hope and vision to the Christian life. Third, the practice of formative preaching and teaching trains the desires through the content of the faith. Finally, all of this results in a life of holiness. The ground of such a life is God. Formative preaching and teaching has in the end but one task—the description of the God witnessed to in the stories of Scripture. Everything else follows after that by coming to rest in the lives of those formed by these stories.

When faith seeks understanding, it is embodied in concrete lives that have been informed by and conformed to the gospel stories through preaching and teaching. These stories and this preaching and teaching provide texture to life as they join head and heart.

## formative preaching and teaching as a practice

Formative preaching and teaching is a habit of a practiced faith. Defining anything as a practice implies that what we believe and what we do cannot be fruitfully separated. It is saying that believing and doing are but two sides of the same reality when each is understood properly. While Jesus walked the earth, He defined two particular means of grace for the Church —baptism and the Lord's Supper. The first is the sign of the new covenant. There is a sense in which the act of baptism turns a person inside out so that profession becomes confession. Those who have become new creatures are baptized so they can be named according to God's reality. The Lord's Supper is the practice of memory and thanksgiving. It is the telling of the story of redemption by enacting the sacrifice made by Christ for us. The Lord's Supper is a concrete action of the grace of God in the Church. Both baptism and the Lord's Supper are practices; that is, they are habits of the heart and mind designed to be means of grace for God's people. They fashion lives around the peculiar stories of the gospel. Our Lord instituted these practices so that we would not be left out on the corner longing for a sign of hope. They are reminders that the One for whom we wait has provided provisions for the interim.

The means of grace that form character extend beyond baptism and the Lord's Supper to other Christian practices. These include prayer, hospitality, public worship, discipleship, the study of Scripture, and formative preaching and teaching. These are all gestures toward the unfolding kingdom of God in history. They reach beyond the realm of theory to touch the heart. As practices they become habits to sustain life and lift our eyes to the hope of the gospel. This is especially true of formative preaching and teaching—a practice that possesses several important characteristics that help establish its significance to our lives.

Formative preaching and teaching is capable of engaging the complexity of life. A number of years ago my wife and I had our first child. We needed to learn an entirely new set of practices in order to be parents. Now after years of child rearing, my wife and I are amazed at just how ignorant we were when we began the parenting journey. But we are equally aware that apart from the specific practices of parenthood, the challenge would have been far too great. Hugs, meals, trips to Disneyland, meetings with teachers—all these things and much more are part of parenthood. In the midst of this, we do not know how we could have survived without the stories and practices of the Christian faith. Just as physical life engages complexity, so does the spiritual life. Concerning this, Paul says, "So then, putting away falsehood, let all of us speak the truth to our neighbors, for we are members of one another" (Eph. 4:25, NRSV). He adds later, "Let no one deceive you with empty words, for because of these things the wrath of God comes on those who are disobedient" (5:6, NRSV). The challenges of the Christian life are complex, and there are many places where falsehood might creep in. Formative preaching and teaching are capable of engaging this complexity and providing us with sufficient resources for growth in grace.

Not only complexity but also coherence characterizes formative preaching and teaching. Connecting the Scriptures with life enables us to make sense of things. Paul says that he came with a new wisdom (2 Cor. 2:6), one that will endure instead of perish. Paul makes this very clear in 2 Cor. 3:4-6:

> Such is the confidence that we have through Christ toward God. Not that we are competent of ourselves to claim anything as coming from us; our competence is from God, who has made us competent to be ministers of a new covenant, not of letter but of spirit; for the letter kills, but the Spirit gives life *(NRSV)*.

This wisdom of a new covenant is coherent because it comes from God. It will ultimately come together to form a life capable of freedom. This is the gift of formative preaching and teaching—it renders life coherent. One conviction of the gospel is that a person who faithfully attends to the preaching and teaching of it will have the resources for a fully coherent life.

A final characteristic of the practice of formative preaching and teaching is that it is realized socially. So much of life in the modern world is lived alone. We live closer to one another than at almost any other time in history, but we have probably never been so alone. Too often people have retreated to privacy, but God did not make us to be alone. Human beings were created for community, and in the Spirit we are called to be the Church. Two powerful word pictures for the Christian life are "body of Christ" and "temple of the Holy Spirit." Both of these are social metaphors. They remind us that God has made us to live together in His kingdom. The discipline of gathering together to hear a sermon or to be taught renders our lives more complete. Paul urges, "Therefore encourage one another with these words" (1 Thess. 4:18, NRSV). The New Testament has many places where the social nature of life is spelled out. Preaching and teaching is a means of grace because it calls the community to find in its common life the resources for a holy life.

These three characteristics (complexity, coherence, and sociality) help to define how formative preaching and teaching is understood as a practice. Children are taught social graces in order to be fit for life together. Learning to say "Thank you," "Excuse me," and "Please" help form a particular kind of life. Such a life is capable of social interaction and enrichment. Through these simple gestures a person begins to lean into the complexity, coherence, and sociality of life. Likewise, being held accountable to formative preaching and teaching begins to prepare a person for what it means to be a Christian. Formative preaching and teaching as a practice forms a life capable of freedom amid the complexity of life through the coherence of the gospel and basic social nature of Christian existence.

## the practice of listening

Formative preaching and teaching requires that we learn how to listen. James urges, "Let everyone be quick to listen" (1:19, NRSV). Modern life is noisy. People on every corner and every channel are calling out for attention. Sometimes it appears that we have lost the capacity for silence. Years of television and radio help dull our senses from the Christian grace of listening. Formative preaching and teaching can serve as training for listening.

Listening is an activity, not an occasion for passivity. After all, communication never works unless it is more than a message. In fact, until the message is heard, it is largely useless. The writer to the Hebrews says, "Therefore we must pay greater attention to what we have heard, so that we do not drift away from it" (2:1, NRSV). When a person is preaching or teaching, the listener is also at work attempting to understand and apply the message. A renewal of formative teaching and preaching will require a renewal of listening.

A very important part of listening is the capacity to focus on what is important. The noise of life presents a sea of words and images that can distract from the truth. Listening is the capacity to locate in the many words and images the ones that matter. Another part of listening is the willingness to

*Listening is the capacity to locate in the many words and images the ones that matter.*

trust. The Scriptures often call for listeners to discern, but more than that it calls for trust. The pace and complexity of life can evoke a fundamental suspicion regarding new ideas. Learning when and how to trust is essential for listening. Still another part of listening is the willingness to act. At a very basic level action is the opening of the mind, but the hope of the gospel is that upon hearing it people will obey. When Paul writes Titus he says, "Teach what is consistent with sound doctrine" (2:1, NRSV). He also uses words such as "tell," "urge," "show yourself," and "declare" in Titus 2 (NRSV). All of these words are double-edged, because they require faithfulness from not only the speaker but also his or her listeners.

Proverbs says, "Fools think their own way is right, but the wise listen to advice" (12:15, NRSV), and "a wise child loves discipline, but a scoffer does not listen to rebuke" (13:1, NRSV). All of this is true because "the teaching of the wise is a fountain of life, so that one may avoid the snares of death" (v. 14, NRSV). Prov. 15:5 adds, "A fool despises a parent's instruction, but the one who heeds admonition is prudent" (NRSV). Listening is essential to the character envisioned by the gospel.

To fully understand listening, it is essential that we give the role of the Holy Spirit fundamental consideration. The Christian faith understands that people respond to formative preaching and teaching because of the work of the Holy Spirit. They are able to listen because of the Holy Spirit's regenerating work in their hearts. Another term for the regenerating work of the Holy Spirit is "prevenient grace." The purpose of prevenient grace is to draw all people to salvation, and it is only by grace that we are able to hear the gospel and respond in faith. The rest of life is an ongoing, timely response to the leadership of the Holy Spirit. At the most basic level this response is listening and as such a life of obedience. Formative preaching and teaching is ineffective unless it arises from the inspiring and empowering work of the Holy Spirit. Accordingly, "It is the spirit that gives life; the flesh is useless. The words that I have spoken to you are spirit and life" (John 6:63, NRSV).

*Formative preaching and teaching is ineffective unless it arises from the inspiring and empowering work of the Holy Spirit.*

## friendship

The practice of preaching and teaching has a long history in the Church. Paul and Peter are biblical examples of powerful preachers. Looking over the history of the Church, other important preachers and teachers have helped to define the Christian faith—people such as Ambrose, Augustine, Aquinas, Luther, and Wesley. More recently, people such as Billy Graham, Phillips Brooks, Karl Barth, and Jurgen Moltmann have graced the Church with preaching and teaching. The preachers and teachers of the Church have inspired students and listeners to greater faith. The life engendered by the ministry of these leaders comes to rest in how they and their listeners responded to the Holy Spirit. This grace of listening takes place as a social practice that occurs through teaching and preaching. All of this makes the case for the importance of friendship.

First and foremost Christian friendship is the recognition of the importance of seeing the grace of God
come to rest in the lives of those we admire. Public
testimonies often inspire younger and less mature
Christians to embody the graces of the faith. The New
Testament describes the friendship between Paul and
Timothy, but a close reading of the concluding re-
marks found in the Epistles names many others. The
role of friendship in the embodying of grace is crucial.
For example, Paul says, "Greet all the brothers and sisters with a holy kiss" (1 Thess. 5:26, NRSV). He also
says, "Greet Prisca and Aquila, and the household of
Onesiphorus" (2 Tim. 4:19, NRSV). Titus 3:13 says,
"Make every effort to send Zenas the lawyer and
Apollos on their way, and see that they lack nothing"
(NRSV). He adds to this, "Greet those who love us in the
faith" (v. 15, NRSV). Col. 4:7 says, "Tychicus will tell you
all the news about me; he is a beloved brother, a faithful minister, and a fellow servant in the Lord" (NRSV).
It seems that the work of Paul was accomplished in
large measure through the friendships engendered
through formative preaching and teaching.

Clearly, formative preaching and teaching fosters
the kind of friendships between teacher and student
or preacher and listener that encourages growth in
grace. Paul expresses a measure of this in 2 Cor. 8:23-
24, "As for Titus, he is my partner and co-worker in
your service; as for our brothers, they are messengers
of the churches, the glory of Christ. Therefore openly
before the churches, show them the proof of your love
and of our reason for boasting about you" (NRSV).

These verses suggest that friendship is important to the ongoing nature of Christian life.

*Friends will encourage, but they will also confront.*

Another thing about formative preaching and teaching is that it allows us to hold a mirror up to our lives. Friends will encourage, but they will also confront. Friends keep us from the boredom of sameness that can lull a person to sleep in life. The writer of Hebrews says, "And let us consider how to provoke one another to love and good deeds, not neglecting to meet together, as is the habit of some, but encouraging one another, and all the more as you see the Day approaching" (10:24-25, NRSV). A couple of chapters later the writer affirms how important others are for living out the Christian life, "since we are surrounded by so great a cloud of witnesses" (12:1, NRSV). Formative preaching and teaching enables friendships to form in the Christian community so that we more fully realize that we need the lives of others to inspire us to greater works of grace. Such friendships help us see ourselves as others do. When a person is in a healthy environment, this "seeing" can be an occasion for deeper spiritual growth. The practice of preaching and teaching is thus also a call to friendship.

The Day of Pentecost was a crucial event for the Early Church. Pentecost tells the story of how a band of nearly defeated believers became dynamic witnesses to the risen Christ. After the demonstrations of the Holy Spirit, Peter stood to preach the first sermon of the Early Church. This was an evangelistic moment, but it was also an occasion for teaching. Peter set forth the basic Christian message that this day was foretold by the prophet Joel. He also asserted that the promise made to David had been fulfilled in the resurrection of Jesus. Peter concluded with these words, "Therefore, let the entire house of Israel know with certainty that God has made him both Lord and Messiah, this Jesus whom you crucified" (Acts 2:36, NRSV). The result of this sermon was the conversion of 3,000 people. Thus began the process of Christian formation that continues to engage the energy of the Church. The faithful practice of formative preaching and teaching continues the faith that was once entrusted to the first believers. It is as we continue to preach and teach the faith that new believers are made mature believers. This is the process of defining and living the "new" wisdom of the gospel so that what was once delivered will be continually practiced.

Henry W. Spaulding II is dean of the School of Arts and Sciences, director of the graduate program in religion, and professor of theology and philosophy at Trevecca Nazarene University. This chapter is an expansion of an article first published in *Holiness Today*, January 2004.